THE ESSENTIAL GUIDE TO
TROUT FISHING

THE ESSENTIAL GUIDE TO
TROUT Fishing

MICHAEL BRANDER

CANONGATE

First published in Great Britain in 1992 by
Canongate Press Plc,
14 Frederick Street
Edinburgh EH2 2HB

British Library Cataloguing-in-Publication Data
A catalogue record for this book is available
on request from The British Library

ISBN 0 86241 395 8

Typeset by Falcon Typographic Art Ltd, Fife, Scotland.
Printed and bound by BPCC Hazell, Aylesbury.

To
my daughter Evelyn Ann,
the finest guddler I know
and
my old friend
Christopher Lethbridge,
as keen a fisherman as they come.

Contents

Preface   9

Introduction   12

Chapter

1 The Modern Scene   17

2 Trout, Their Habitat and Habits   21

3 The Tackle   39

4 Initial Dry Practice and Preparation   54

5 Artificial Flies, Lures and Baits
  and Their Presentation   67

6 Trout Behaviour and Catching Them   84

7 Different Waters Different Approaches   99

8 Mainly Lochs, Lakes and Reservoirs   122

9 Mainly Small Rivers   131

Recipes   139

Glossary of Terms   140

Further Reading   143

Preface

In a previous book on trout fishing I restricted myself mainly to fly fishing, both wet and dry, since this is the way the majority of sporting anglers try to catch trout. There are occasions, however, when spinning and bait fishing for trout and even worming are the only methods likely to catch trout in the prevailing conditions. It is also a fact that clear-water upstream worming can be as delicate an art as up-stream nymphing and indeed is an almost identical method of fishing.

Simply dangling a worm in a muddy pool at the end of a spate may also be a profitable way of catching trout. There are occasions when fishing in this way may be the only feasible way to catch a trout with a rod and line and may be acceptable on those grounds, but it is not in the same sporting league as clear-water up-stream worming. The latter is an art while the former can be very close to slaughter and (dependent on the bylaws) may be rightly classified as illegal, along with certain baits and other more obvious forms of law-breaking such as dynamiting or netting a pool, or poisoning it with cyanide. There is another distinction, however; that all the latter are methods of large-scale poaching and, particularly in the case of cyanide, are likely to affect fish stocks for years to come.

There are still some bigoted dry fly specialists who dismiss wet fly fishing with the time-worn phrase that it is merely a 'chuck-it-and-chance-it' method of fishing. Yet these same individuals will usually happily turn to up-stream nymphing when their favourite method of fishing is not possible. To suggest to them that up-stream worming is as difficult an art would be regarded as heresy. The truth is that there are times and places when any of the various methods of catching trout described are more suitable than the others. For instance faced with a small Scottish burn and without either rod or line it is still possible to provide oneself with a delicious plateful of trout in a short time by guddling, i.e. catching them by feeling for them under stones with the hands. Like learning to snare rabbits, guddling is something most Scots country children learn when they are young and in the process they also learn unconsciously to know where trout are likely to lie. This in turn prepares them for fishing those same burns later with rod and line and the knowledge gained then is just as useful subsequently in larger rivers.

I have to confess that I have never been a particularly expert guddler, but after introducing my younger daughter to the art she was soon providing us regularly with bags of twenty or thirty small trout of a quarter to half a pound from our local burn. Fishing with a fly and with all the skill I could muster I was usually lucky if I achieved half that number. Eventually this scourge of the local burn grew up and moved on and now it is left to more orthodox anglers to keep the numbers of smaller trout within bounds. At the worst now the wet and dry fly exponents only have to vie with up-stream worming and nymphing, or with natural predators such as herons and occasional otters, apart from that villainous introduction, the mink.

This short guide is intended as introduction for anyone who is contemplating taking up trout fishing. It can be no more than an introduction for the only way to learn to catch trout is by practice and observation with or without rod and line. It does, however, attempt to outline the various methods of fishing for trout; the tackle and other equipment required and how to use it; the various kinds of trout which may be caught and their habits and habitat; as well as the best ways of approaching the sport so as to obtain the maximum pleasure from it. Although the same rule applies to many sports other than fishing, unfortunately people often become so obsessed with particular aspects of the sport that they tend to forget it should be first and foremost a pleasure.

Fortunately there are probably more people willing to provide tuition today than there have ever been and in addition there is undoubtedly more fishing available.

With diversification increasingly essential in agriculture, more and more farmers with a natural water supply available have turned to rearing trout and providing angling facilities, frequently including board and tuition as part of a package deal. There are also many sporting hotels which offer fishing holidays with tuition by experts. Then again there are numerous angling clubs throughout the country, although many of the best have a long waiting list for membership.

With home videos and TV documentaries as well as books the would-be angler is inundated with advice today, but there is still scope for this kind of short guide. Even after successfully being taught the basics of trout fishing, casting, playing and netting a trout, on a holiday course it is always useful to have a guide on hand to consult at leisure. There are invariably small points which slip the memory in course of time, or which are omitted by the most expert of tutors, that may be referred to later. More importantly, perhaps, such a guide may keep alive in the novice angler's mind the satisfaction to be had from trout fishing and also open up fresh possibilities to help him, or her, to obtain the maximum fulfilment from their sport.

Finally, my thanks are due to numerous people for the tedious business of reading and commenting on the manuscript, notably Mr James Muirhead of John Dickson & Son, the well-known gunsmith and fishing tackle dealer of Frederick Street, Edinburgh, my son, Andrew Michael, and Mr K.H. Grose, but for any errors, or omissions, I am solely responsible.

Introduction

Where to Start
For the absolute beginner who is wondering about taking up fishing the question of where to start can be something of a stumbling block. Does one go to a fishing shop, ask for advice and buy tackle; does one take one of those holiday courses often to be seen advertised in fishing journals at a 'fishery', usually attached to what is claimed to be a well-known fishing inn, where one is assured of receiving expert coaching; does one join a fishing club and hope the members will provide advice, does one simply buy a book or video and carry on from there; or is it best perhaps to consider more than one of these options. A lot depends on the time available, the degree of commitment, and of course the individual temperament.

Four Starting Points
1 The Fishing Tackle Shop
There are of course those who having decided to start fishing will immediately enter a fishing tackle shop, equip themselves with expensive gear and sally forth to the river or loch, only then to discover there is rather more to it all than being equipped as the *parfait* angler'. Furthermore, although reputable fishing tackle salesmen will go to the trouble of helping the beginner, advising him as to what he will and will not need initially and where he should go to get lessons, there are those will simply look on him as a gift from the gods and sell him a great deal of tackle which it is doubtful he will ever need or use. Even an experienced angler can easily lose his head when browsing in a tackle shop and leave with much that he really does not need, having spent more than he should. At some point, however, the beginner will have to buy tackle and provided that he restricts himself to the minimum required and asks advice regarding clubs and tuition, as

well as perhaps on suitable books, the fishing tackle shop can be one way of getting started.

2 Holiday Tuition

More cautious novices may decide to take one of the many holiday breaks advertised regularly in fishing journals at a 'fishery' and, if their choice is sound, benefit from the coaching of expert fishermen. Fishing journals such as the *Angling Times*, *Trout & Salmon*, or *Trout Fisherman*, tend to have occasional articles suitable for novices, but for the large part are preaching to the converted, or catering for the knowledgeable. Although they may contain material useful to the novice and sufficient to whet his appetite for more, their most valuable asset to the beginner probably lies in the advertisements offering tuition which they contain, most of which are likely to be genuine enough. Many of these offer to provide tackle for the beginner either on hire, or loan, or on sale in their own shop, so that this can be a satisfactory way of starting from scratch.

3 The Fishing Club

A third method of approach for the novice may be to join a local trout fishing club. There are clubs of this type in most sizeable towns close to any good fishing waters and though many have a long waiting list there are usually some that are happy to have new members and the reputable fishing tackle shop will usually be able to give the novice the address of the secretary. This in turn can usually lead to advice on obtaining tuition.

4 Books and Videos

Another obvious first step is to buy a book such as this, which is designed to show the beginner what to look for and what to avoid, as well as giving some idea of the pleasures and satisfactions to be obtained from trout fishing in its many forms. Buying a book is still obviously the least expensive choice for the non-committed beginner. Rather more expensive, but often very satisfactory, may be one of the many videos to be had on trout fishing. In that it is both cheaper and easier to refer to for any particular point, however, the book probably still has the edge over the video even today.

The Essence of Trout Fishing
Yet it must be stressed that trout fishing is not just a 'hobby', or a pastime: it should not be regarded as on a par with stamp collecting. At its worst it is an obsession and a full-time occupation; at best, once learned, it is a consuming interest, a testing skill and an enjoyable sport which totally alters the way one looks at water, whether smooth mill pond, wave-capped loch, highland river running high and drumly, or clear chalk stream in southern England. The urge to catch a fish on rod and line, once learned, is something never forgotten.

The Variety
The attraction of trout fishing lies to a large extent in the widely varied places it may take the angler as well as the different methods necessary to catch them. The chalk streams surrounded by lush Hampshire water meadows where large trout feeding serenely in the clear glass-like water must be stalked with care (and where only a dry fly can be employed to any effect) can be very satisfying in their way. In violent contrast is a small lochan, five or more miles from the nearest road, surrounded by rugged Highland mountains where almost any wet fly may at times catch a full bag of small wild brown trout. Yet each may provide unforgettable sport for the same fisherman.

The Specialists
Do not be misled by those who claim that their method of catching trout is infinitely preferable to any other, whether it be the dry fly enthusiast, the water temperature fanatic, or the bait casting madman. There are always those in every sport who insist that 'their' sporting methods are the best, such as the gundog enthusiast who can see no good in other breeds, the car fetishist who knows that there is no other make than his, and so on. Specialists in any sport may be enthusiastic, but they miss more than half the fun. The variety to be had in trout fishing, and the enjoyment from the immensely different surroundings in which it can

take place accounts for more than half its appeal. The keen fisherman should be able to fish with a wet fly, dry fly, and even a worm with equal facility, and when necessary or desirable should be able to use a spinning rod to good effect. If the same angler is also capable of guddling trout, so much the better.

The Water

Just as there is more than one way to cook a trout so there are many ways to catch them, and the waters in which trout may be found are also extremely varied. These are, however, sometimes classified simply as Still-water and Flowing-water. The distinction is that the former has little or no discernable current whereas the latter has a clear and distinct rate of flow. The former may vary from man-made gravel pits, or artificial ponds scooped out by bulldozers, to large reservoirs, lakes and lochs. The latter covers all sorts and conditions of river from languid clear chalk streams winding amongst southern water meadows, through the impressive waters of major tributaries such as the Thames, the Severn, the Clyde, or the Tay, to the rushing waters of some upland brook or burn. The surroundings of the water, as much as the water itself may make up a good part of the fisherman's enjoyment of each day, but it is the fish which are the quarry and it is catching them which ultimately makes the experience memorable.

Peace Not Patience

In absorbing the peaceful pace of the countryside, or breathing the wonderfully bracing air of the highlands, in concentrating the mind solely on catching fish, in forgetting for the time involved in fishing all the cares and worries of everyday life, the angler unconsciously gains an inner peace and satisfaction not as readily obtained in any other sport. Do not innocently imagine that patience has anything to do with it, as so many people who know nothing of fishing often patronisingly assume. Patience may be a virtue but it is one that not many anglers possess, and it is not a necessary feature of fishing. It is the fishing and catching of fish which concentrates the mind.

Fly Fishing and Spinning

There are a number of different approaches to catching trout, which will be noted in due course, but basically there are two main methods. These are either by casting with a fly rod, with wet or dry fly or lure, from a bank, by wading, or from a boat, which may also be said to cover subsidiary forms of fishing such as dapping, up-stream nymphing and similar methods, or by bait casting with a spinning rod, which may be said to include trolling with a minnow from a boat. There are also various other methods of catching trout, with a worm, with maggots, or with the bare hands. Each form of fishing has its firm advocates and each may be suited to certain times and places. The two main methods of fishing are quite different, as is the tackle employed; details of each are duly noted and dealt with in subsequent chapters, as are the other forms of fishing mentioned.

The First Trout

Whether fishing with fly or spinning, no book can ever truly prepare the beginner for that wonderful feeling of being in touch with the very first trout or that heart-stopping moment when it is truly hooked, when the rod is bending unbelievably and the reel is screaming as the line runs off it at amazing speed leaving one wondering if this can really be true. Nor can a book capture the feeling of sheer blissful fulfillment when that first trout has been satisfactorily netted and is lying on the bank, its scales glittering and spots shining. There is then inevitably a moment of regret as there must always be on such occasions. No book can ever quite capture such moments but it can provide sound advice on preparation and practice. After that first trout there are many ways the novice angler can set about enjoying good and varied sport and here at least a book can point the beginner in the right directions. That is what this book sets out to do.

CHAPTER ONE

The Modern Scene

The Season

In one important detail trout fishing has greatly changed in the past two decades. Before the advent of 'put and take' fishing, with artificially bred fish being introduced into enclosed waters from special breeding pens in neighbouring fish farms throughout the year, the natural breeding cycle controlled fishing seasons. From around October to around April there was a close season when fish were allowed to breed in peace, and when indeed they were so out of condition, lean and dark-coloured, that they were simply not worth catching. Today artificially bred rainbow trout may be caught at almost any time. The main controlling factor appears to be the weather since few people wish to catch fish during the colder months from November through to February and March. On such commercial waters it is advisable, however, to check beforehand when fishing is permitted, as well as the rules laid down as to how fish may be caught, which may also vary with different fisheries. On less commercialised waters, where fish farming does not reign supreme, the seasons still hold sway.

The Maharajah's Fishing

In the India of the 1930s when some of the Maharajahs with vast incomes had reached heights of decadence at which the Western press marvelled, there was one who had a large jewelled throne installed above a comparatively small pool surrounded by exotic orchids and richly perfumed plants. When his obese majesty had been settled on his throne he would be handed a fishing rod already baited with a fish pellet on a hook and a large hand-reared trout from his well-stocked fish ponds would be introduced into the pool. At the first cast the unwary beast, accustomed to feeding on just such pellets, would seize the bait and would be duly played by the pudgy royal angler. It would finally be netted by one of the attendant houris to the applause of her companions. Exhausted by such outdoor exertions the Maharajah then retired to his harem. This was cited at the time as an example of Eastern decadence and the nadir of sportsmanship. There is, sadly, very little difference between this and some of the less savoury practices prevalent in certain commercialised waters today.

Fish Farming

Different varieties of trout are widespread throughout the world, particularly in Europe, North America, New Zealand and parts of Africa. Because they are easily bred in fish farms an immense explosion in numbers has taken place during the post-war decades, but particularly since the 1970s onwards. The principle of breeding fish in controlled surroundings and inducing rapid artificial growth through intensive feeding has only become widespread during the past two decades.

Put and Take Fishing

The custom of 'put and take' fishing as it is descriptively termed, has inevitably followed. In its crudest form, in parts of the USA, a 'fisherman' selects a fish from an aquarium glass-sided tank from which it is netted. It is then placed in an artificial pool, the 'fisherman' is handed a baited rod which he then casts into the pool and the fish, accustomed to being fed on the artificial bait placed on the hook, at once seizes the 'food' thus presented. It is played, netted, and the 'fisherman' can pose for his photograph with his catch, which is then either returned to the tank to repeat the process or is despatched, then packed in ice for the 'sportsman' to take home in triumph. In the ultimate scenario the 'fisherman' may also have a plaster cast made and display a replica of the monster in a glass cabinet in his 'den'. This merely costs a little more. By comparison with this the Maharajah was an also-ran.

Stocking the Water

Not all artificial stocking of fishing water is either quite so crude or quite so unsporting as this ultimate form of commercialisation, yet it may still merit the description 'put and take' where stocks are replenished at frequent intervals. When fish are reared and let loose in natural waters, such as a lake or brook, where they may still be artificially fed at times but are allowed to adapt to a wild existence, matters are not necessarily unfairly balanced against the fish. They learn to adapt quickly enough and such fish may not only become hard to catch, but also well worth catching, putting up a strong fight so that with a bag limit and a minimum size limit this may provide reasonable sporting fishing. This may still be termed loosely 'put and take' fishing because, when a number have been caught, they may be replaced by a corresponding number of fresh fish.

Re-stocking

It has, of course, been the practice for many years to re-stock fishing waters, whether a river or a lake, and in effect there is very little difference between this and much 'put and take' fishing. The fishery owners, whether angling clubs, riparian owners acting in unison, or individuals, have in effect been doing little more than replenishing stocks. The only real difference today is that with modern methods of breeding and feeding, the fish can be more readily replaced and kept in greater numbers than would have been practical in previous years so that the results may be very much more spectacular, both in size of fish and numbers available.

The Dangers

On the whole this should be nothing but good news for the fisherman, but of course it is open to abuse, as indicated above, and unless carefully controlled it can also lead to overstocking and disease. Careful management is essential and stocks can easily be wiped out at various stages by pollution, disease or predators. Fish farming is not as simple as it might seem at first sight. In the hands of unscrupulous or careless operators the system is very obviously not only open to abuse but can have disastrous consequences for others when disease arises. Unfortunately it can also have disastrous effects on those who fish. Having never really had to learn about fish and their habits, or how to fish with a fly, or the ethics of sportsmanship involved, some modern anglers used only to commercial waters consider it a matter of simplicity to catch fish. As yet I have not heard of any establishments in this country prepared to provide the individual fish to be caught by their patrons as in the USA but there do seem to be some people who share the Maharajah's ideas on fishing.

Barbless Hooks and Bag Limits
There are commercial fisheries where it is possible to take and return as many fish over and above the bag limit as may be caught with barbless hooks, but if they are simple to catch, however large they may be, this begins to pall after a while. The fact is that fishing should never be too easy, for without requiring a fair degree of concentration and effort it ceases to be worthwhile.

Faced with the alternative of catching a tame eight-pounder in such circumstances or a wild half-pounder in a small Scottish burn there should be no question which anyone who aspires to be an honest angler would choose. After catching and returning the same or a similar eight-pounder a dozen times or more even the most ardent angler might find the experience a little boring.

CHAPTER TWO

Trout, Their Habitat and Habits

The Many Differences
The innocent beginner might imagine that one trout is exactly like another, but few things could be further from the truth. It is almost true to say that trout may vary as much as humans, in shape, size and type, colouration and, if not brains, at least in experience. The fish living in heavily fished waters soon learns to reject the obvious lures and the ill-cast flies which might readily attract any fish in virgin waters. The European Brook or Brown trout may vary in size and colouration according to the feed available and the surroundings in which it lives. Even the flesh may vary from a glorious pinky colour to a dark grey-white. The American Brook trout and the Rainbow trout are as different from them as they in turn may be from each other.

The Variants
Then there are variants such as Sea trout and cannibal, or Ferox, trout. The former are a trout which, as the name implies, go out to sea, like the salmon, and return to their native rivers to spawn. They are mainly caught in the late evening or early morning and can provide a fascinating fight with silvery explosions as they break the surface and leap frantically at the end of the line in an effort to shake free the hook. The latter live at greater depths than the ordinary trout and grow to an enormous size. It must be obvious then that trout can vary not just in size, shape and colouration, but in their habits and behaviour too. Anyone who has seen an ill-shaped Ferox with a great hooked cannibal jaw and lean, dark body would barely associate it with a small, neat, well-formed Brown trout.

The Various Species
Sea Trout
Salmo trutta trutta, or Sea trout, range in size from 16 inches to 30 inches or more, and are found widely throughout Europe, Asia and North Africa. As the name implies they live primarily in the sea and move up-river from June through to October to breed, like salmon, in the gravel spawning beds in the headwaters, returning to the sea as spent fish. They can provide immensely sporting fishing and are usually best fished for in the late evening and early morning when they are on the move.

Brook Trout or Brown Trout
Salmo trutta fario, the Brook or Brown trout, range usually from around 6 inches in small brooks, or where the feeding is poor, to as much as 22 inches or even more. Despite the name they also frequent lakes or lochs or any fresh water to which they can gain access. They were originally only found in Europe, but have been artificially introduced in large quantities around the world, particularly in the USA, New Zealand and parts of Africa, where they are now widely distributed. They are easily bred and introduced into new water.

American Brook Trout
Salvelinus Fontenalis, or American Brook trout are really speckled char, not trout at all, although closely resembling them and generally ranging in size from 15 to 18 inches. These have long been introduced into numerous European waters and may provide very good sport.

Rainbow Trout
Salmo irideus, or Rainbow trout, grow as large as 27 inches. They originated in Californian coastal waters but have been widely introduced to inland waters throughout the USA, Europe, New Zealand and East Africa. Like other species, they breed in running water but spawn in the spring. They are readily reared in fish farms and are farmed in enormous numbers in Europe and the USA. They can provide exciting sport and are the mainstay of most 'put

and take' fisheries. They are frequently fished for with large, brightly coloured lures, or streamers, which have little or no relation to any natural fly or trout feed. This has been criticised by some as an unnatural, debased form of fishing but anyone who has fished for mackerel with rod and line should recognise a similarity, and in some circumstances it may be the only way to catch the fish.

Ferox

Salmo ferox is a fine example of the effects of feed and habitat on trout growth. Originally thought to be a separate specimen, the Ferox has long been recognised as merely a cannibal variant. In lochs such as Loch Awe, where char abound, these trout start as cannibals eating smaller trout. As they grow larger so they tend to swim deeper and it is then they start feeding on the char, which live in shoals at a lower depth than the average trout. The char prove easier prey and the cannibal trout, already grown large, now move downwards to feed at an even greater depth, and from then on can attain very large proportions indeed. Ferox of over twenty pounds are common, but they are often ill-shaped with large heads, grotesquely hooked jaws, and long lean bodies. In fairness it must be added that some can also be very handsome specimens. Virtually the only method of catching them, however, is by trolling, or spinning, a large bait at considerable depth.

Other Species

Other recognised species of trout include the well known Loch Leven trout, *Salmo levenensis*, originating, as the name implies in Loch Leven, from whence it has been introduced all round the world and is famed for its hard fighting qualities. The Sewen, or Western trout, *Salmo cambricus*, also known as the White trout, is found in Wales, as well as Norway and Denmark. Another type of trout found in Wales is the Welsh Black-Finned trout, *Salmo nigripinnis*, which as the name indicates has dark coloured fins, that are sometimes nearly black, The Phinock, or Eastern Sea trout, *Salmo brachypoma*, is a migratory species which is found in the Forth and Tay and as far north as the Moray Firth. In Ireland there is the remarkable, very red-coloured Gillaroo, *Salmo stomachicus*, notable for the thickness of its stomach wall, thought to be caused by its diet of molluscs although other mollusc-eating fish do not have the same characteristic.

Habitat
While fresh water is obviously the requisite habitat for trout of all sorts, this may come in many forms. The ideal is probably a river in the gravelly headwaters of which the female trout lays its eggs, and in which the trout itself grows to maturity, completing the natural cycle by spawning or fertilising the eggs to perpetuate the species. The habitat, however, may vary from small, man-made ponds, or large lakes or reservoirs, completely landlocked, which are periodically stocked with young fry from fish farms, to fast-flowing rivers or lochs running to the sea, where Brown and even Rainbow trout may be found alongside Sea trout in the brackish waters.

Growth Rate
The amount of alkaline or acid contained in any water determines to a very large extent the size of the trout to be found in it. Waters with a high alkaline content, commonly encountered in limestone or chalk-based land, will be found to contain a healthy population of insects and plant life, as well as edible crustacea such as crayfish and shrimps on which the trout will thrive. The converse applies, of course, in waters with a noticeable acid content, commonly found in moorland, or peaty soils, where insect and plant life finds it hard to establish itself and is usually nothing like so readily available. Other forms of feeding for fish may also be lacking. The fish in alkaline waters tend therefore to have a much higher growth rate than those in acid waters.

The Effects of Acid Rain
Carried to the ultimate degree, waters with a very high acid content, as for instance those badly affected by acid rain, will have no trout at all since there is no natural feeding available in the form of insect or plant life.

Adding lime to such waters may bring down the acid content and permit fish to survive and even breed, but may also harm many other forms of mammal and plant life. A satisfactory solution has not yet been found to this problem.

Flow Rate

The rate of flow of the water is another major feature affecting the trout's growth rate. On the whole the faster the water flow the slower the growth rate of the trout, since, in general, there is less available to eat. Plant life and small crustacea are unlikely to be found in areas with a very fast rate of flow, preferring the sheltered areas, where the water is comparatively calm. Similarly trout will invariably be found in any waters in areas where they can find the most food with the least expenditure of effort. Like the plant life and crustacea, the trout in fast-flowing waters will be found in the sheltered areas provided by rocks or backwaters. The trout in these fast-flowing rivers naturally have a harder task to survive so it is readily understandable that they seldom grow to anything like the same size as those in sheltered waters. Inevitably, therefore, a great deal depends on the water in which a trout is forced to live, but the smaller, hardier trout which has been forced to spend its life in a fast flowing river or stream may well prove a fine fighting fish. It may also be far more difficult to catch, and far more worth catching, than a fish twice or more its size which has spent its entire life in the placid water of a millpond or similar enclosed area, especially one reared in a commercial fishery with no experience of life in the wild.

The Types of Fishing Water

There are, roughly speaking, only four major categories of fishing water. These are first, and most obviously, the larger and better known rivers, followed secondly by the larger lakes, lochs and man-made reservoirs. Third are the smaller lochs, lakes and artificial ponds, including numerous gravel pits, which are to be found in many areas. Last there are the many smaller rivers, streams and burns, found all over the country. Included in both first and last categories are the chalk streams, which provide a very different form of fishing. As noted, the second and third categories, where there is no immediately obvious flow of water, are sometimes lumped together as stillwater fishing, as opposed to the others where the rate of flow is plain, but there are clearly many variations.

The Major Rivers
The more famous of these, such as the Avon, the Wye, the Tay and the Tweed, are well known for more than their excellence as fishing rivers. They are physical and geographical features steeped in the history of the countryside through which they flow. Rain-fed from numerous feeder subsidiaries throughout their length, they may be as much as fifty or more yards across and subject to floods which may more than double their width in some areas. They may be fished by wading, or from boats, or from the bank, but they will inevitably have their periods when the water is either too low to fish, or in flood and too high and muddy.

The Larger Lakes, Reservoirs and Lochs
The two former provide a great deal of the fishing to be had in England and Wales, and the two latter provide some excellent fishing in Scotland and Ireland. These also may generally be fished by boat, or from the banks, or water's edge. The former, especially, are often artificially stocked with brown and rainbow trout. The latter may be artificially stocked, but are more frequently reliant on natural re-stocking or on escapees from fish farms rather than on deliberate policy.

The Smaller Lakes and Lochs
Whether natural or artificial—or a combination of the two, as in the case of gravel pits turned into fisheries—such smaller areas of water may provide very good sport. The small hill loch, or little, seldom-fished lake may be able to rely on natural stocks of fish, but the majority of these small waters are artificially stocked. Whether stocked on a

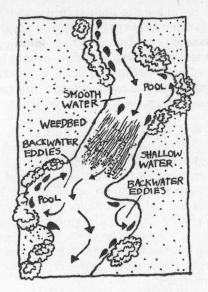

A TYPICAL LOWLAND STREAM

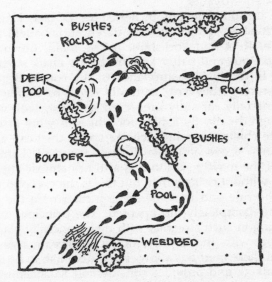

A TYPICAL HIGHLAND STREAM

yearly basis, or on a more regular 'put-and-take' principle (sometimes as often as every two or three days) such waters may provide some excellent sport. Anything more than a few acres in size may well be fished from a boat, as well as from the edge. Whether the sport is good or bad may depend as much on the management, the trout stocked, and the surroundings, as on the water itself.

The Smaller Rivers, Streams and Burns
There are numerous small rivers, streams and burns to be found throughout the length and breadth of the country which may or may not be artificially stocked, and which can provide surprisingly good sport for the keen angler. It may be that the fish are smaller and that they have to be stalked carefully, but the pleasure of catching a bag of wary small trout may well be every bit as great as that of catching a bag limit of larger and tamer reared trout which have never really learned to distinguish a live fly from its artificial counterpart.

The Chalk Streams
These are found mostly in Berkshire, Dorset, Hampshire and Wiltshire, with a few scattered as far afield as Derbyshire, Kent and Yorkshire. In the main, however, the more famous and better known dry fly chalk streams are found in the lush pasturelands of the south. Because of their scarcity they are, naturally enough, highly prized and generally carefully preserved and very well stocked. Although the dry fly fishing for which they are famed can provide challenging and delicate sport, they can also, on occasions, prove almost a duffer's paradise. During the start of the mayfly season it is at times almost impossible to cast without rising a fish, but this is the exception rather than the rule and in some areas furthermore the mayfly has now completely disappeared. The principal methods of fishing in such streams, with their generally glass-clear water, is with the dry fly, or by up-stream nymphing. Each of these methods allows individual fish to be marked and stalked, and provides considerable satisfaction to the angler, but the same can be as true of other methods of fishing in less highly prized waters.

'Grey' Areas

There are certain waters in which trout may be found where there is occasional man-made current. Thus mill-streams, governed by weirs, may be totally without any current until the weirs are opened. In the same way rivers governed by hydro-electric schemes may be subject to a periodic regular spate, raising and lowering the water several feet. Finally, canals on which there is regular traffic may have a noticeable current when there is considerable movement of barges resulting in the lock gates frequently opening and closing.

Possible Variations in Appearance of Trout

Although trout living in similar habitats might be expected to resemble each other, this is far from the case. Even trout caught in the same loch or reservoir may be entirely different. Those at one end might have been living on a muddy bottom, consuming mainly worms, crustacea and similar food sifted from the silt; the resulting fish might be dark coloured and eel-shaped with white flesh. A trout from the other end of the same loch living on a totally different diet, surviving as a surface feeder mainly on flies and insects, might well be full-bellied and golden coloured with finely marked spots on its flanks. The flesh of such a trout may be pink rather than white.

Variations in Reaction

However well stocked and however attractive the sur-roundings of any fishing water may be, there is no doubt that the reactions of the trout to the fly cast over it make a great deal of difference to the angler's sport. The hand-reared trout, no matter what the species or size, which has been fed on pellets all its life, may play well enough when it has been hooked, and may look a handsome prize when it has been landed, but the sporting angler must question whether that is enough. The trout that knows no difference between a poorly cast fly and the real thing is an innocent abroad waiting for the slaughter. This is a very different trout from its counterpart which has been bred and survived in the wild, whether river or loch. Such a trout may not be as handsome a catch, but will certainly prove harder to catch and make victory that much more rewarding.

The Common Factors
Whether reared on a fish farm or a natural product of the wild, whether a simple innocent awaiting its fate, or a wise and hardened specimen with many years' experience in rejecting artificial flies and lures, there are certain features that each of these fish has in common.

Vision
The field of vision of either fish is limited specifically to a small area above its head. In general it may therefore be anticipated that in a river or stream the trout will be facing any current and looking up-stream, since it is from that direction their food is likely to appear. Yet while their field of vision is certainly restricted it may include the bank of a river, so it is not advisable to stand in full view of the water on the bank of a river or lake. Nor is it advisable to allow a moving shadow to fall on the water.

Hearing
It should also be borne in mind that a trout is acutely sensitive to vibration, so that when fishing in a boat it is inadvisable to splash around with the oars, or, for instance, to knock out a pipe on the boat itself, or, above all, to have a radio blasting out music. Nor is it a good plan to stamp heavily around on the bank when approaching the water on foot, or to splash around in waders.

The Effect of Disturbance
It is only necessary to watch through polaroid spectacles from a height above an angler wading upstream to see how easily the trout are disturbed by incautious movements, by careless noisy wading, by the shadow cast by the angler, by the sight of the line flashing above them or splashing on the water after a poorly executed cast. Any of these are enough to cause the trout to disappear from sight, whereas previously they might have been seen lying head to the current in considerable numbers. It is always desirable to move carefully when fishing.

Water Temperature

Water temperature will, of course also affect matters considerably. Outside atmospheric conditions may drive fish deeper, just as warmer conditions will generally tend to bring them to the surface. An imminent snow storm may perversely raise the water temperature so that fish are actually rising and being caught in near blizzard conditions when hitherto they have refused to rise all day. It has to be appreciated that water temperature is liable to considerable variations, more especially in still water where there is no current to keep it colder.

The Effect of Sun on Water Layers

The effect of sun on large expanses of water is to heat the bottom, as the sun's rays pass through the water. This in turn heats the water itself. The heated layer of water next to the bottom rises replacing the colder layer above. Cold water is denser and heavier than warm water which rises accordingly through the colder water. There is therefore constant change in water temperature in the various layers of the water. Naturally the deeper the water the slower it tends to heat, but the longer it retains the heat. When the upper layer of water is warm the fish tend to rise to the surface. The heated layers of water also affect the life cycles of the various flies on which the trout feed, causing them to feed at different depths.

Effects of Sun, Depth and Wind

In the summer months the warmth of the sun usually penetrates any large stretch of water warming it by degrees and, in the upper layers nearest the surface, encouraging minute food growth on which the trout thrive. During a prolonged warm period this upper layer of water increases, but except in very shallow waters there is generally a lower layer to which the sun never penetrates and which remains permanently cold and dark. Between the two areas is an important transitional layer known as the thermocline. For much of the year the larger waters have these three distinct layers, the warmer feeding area above the thermocline, the thermocline itself and the lower, colder and darker layer beneath. The effects of a heavy storm of wind and rain can be temporarily to mix the three areas; during the autumn gales this is what happens so that during the winter months there is no discernible difference in the water at various depths. The effect of wind may also be to drive the feeding layer towards the shore on which it is blowing. The thermocline then tilts and the feeding layer is far deeper on one side of the lake, loch or reservoir than on the other. Thus, as any experienced angler knows, the feeding on the lee shore will be better and the trout will congregate there.

The Effects of Light and Shade
During very sunny weather the plankton tend to move downwards towards the thermocline, away from the surface and nearer the darker, shadier depths. In clear waters, therefore, it is reasonable to expect the trout to be feeding quite deep down on a sunny day, whereas towards nightfall they will tend to come gradually nearer to the surface. In the hours of darkness in midsummer there will be a lot of surface, or near-surface activity. In murkier waters, however, they will tend not to feed so deeply and may be caught at shallower depths accordingly, but again they will tend to come closer to the surface as the evening approaches or during a dull and overcast day.

The Effects of Prolonged Hot Weather
Prolonged hot weather can have considerable effects on the feeding habits of trout. As noted, it can cause considerable growth of weed and plant life near the surface resulting in oxygen starvation of the fish in the water. In comparatively shallow enclosed waters the growth of algae can eventually turn the water green and the fish will simply die from lack of oxygen. Where there is deep water, however, the larger fish normally found there may be forced closer to the surface again because of lack of oxygen deeper down caused by all the detritus of the richer feeding sinking to the bottom.

Atmospheric Pressure
During thundery weather the heavy atmospheric pressure causes fish to become lethargic and they cease to feed

near the surface. The surface water is depleted of oxygen and this drives the fish down deeper to where there is more oxygen in the water. They are likely to be feeding either fairly deep or on the bottom, if at all, during such conditions. Weather conditions can thus greatly affect the feeding habits and movements of the fish, so that no two days even on the same water are likely to be precisely identical.

Diet
Natural Trout Food
The natural feeding for a trout is primarily based on water-bred insect life; the larvae of the ephemeridae; the larvae or caddis of the sedge flies and of gnats; and the chironomus as well as the mature forms of these insects, the duns, spinners and sedge flies. Freshwater shrimps, snails and small bivalves and worms are also eagerly eaten. They will also turn to small fish such as minnows, stickle-backs, alevins, trout-fry and loaches or even chub if they are present. Less obvious sources of food are insects blown off the land, or from bushes, trees and similar vegetation by the bankside; alder flies, bluebottles, dragon flies, wasps, bees, beetles, grasshoppers, even small mice and frogs may be taken by hungry trout.

The Natural Flies or Ephemeridae
There are certain times of the day throughout the year in every area when insects of one kind or another may be seen to be particularly attractive to trout. The morning and evening 'rise' when trout are seen feeding particularly voraciously, are common to most waters. There is also what is known as the 'Duffer's Fortnight' on the chalk streams of the south when mayflies are hatching and the trout seem to go mad, leaping frantically after every hatching mayfly they can see. There are times, such as these, when skill is scarcely necessary and when even the complete novice casting extremely badly is likely to catch a trout with almost every cast. There are other times, as every fisherman knows, to be experienced on every water, when fish are apparently rising freely and taking some sort of fly, but when they refuse to take anything even the most

a) FEMALE SPINNERS LAY THEIR EGGS IN WATER

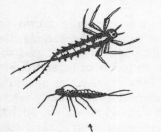

b) NYMPHS WITH RUDIMENTARY
WINGCASES HATCH FROM
THE EGGS

c) AS THE NYMPHS MATURE, THEIR
WINGCASES DEVELOP FULLY

d) THE NYMPHS RISE TO THE
SURFACE TO HATCH

e) DUNS HATCH AND
TAKE FLIGHT

above and opposite THE LIFE CYCLE OF THE AQUATIC FLY

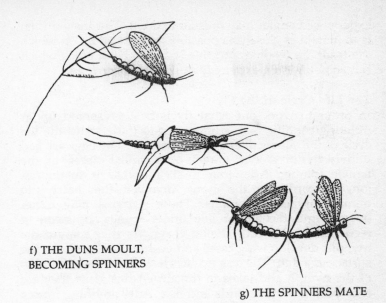

**f) THE DUNS MOULT,
BECOMING SPINNERS**

g) THE SPINNERS MATE

**h) THE SPINNER FEMALES LAY
THEIR EGGS BY
(i) DROPPING CLUSTERS;
(ii) RELEASING GROUPS OF
TWO OR THREE;
(iii) LAYING UNDERWATER**

(i)

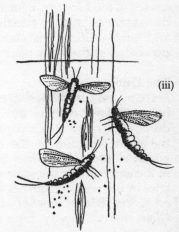

(iii)

(ii)

experienced angler may present to them. The answer then is to imitate as closely as possible the natural fly on which the trout are feeding, but this is a stumbling block which can sometimes be extremely difficult to overcome.

The Life Cycle of the Fly
In order to work out what fly is best presented under differing conditions it is important to understand the life cycle of the aquatic flies or ephemeridae. The eggs are laid underwater on stones, gravel, or in similar places, by the female spinner. After four to six months, or sometimes longer according to the species involved, they hatch into minute larvae or nymphs. These nymphs may either burrow into the silt or live under stones, or swim in reed beds or beneath similar cover. As they mature the nymphs develop wing cases and eventually struggle to the surface as a dun. The dun extracts itself from the larval skin of the nymph and takes to the air. At this stage they are easy prey to waiting birds and fish. After anything from a few hours to a few days depending on the species the duns finally moult and turn into spinners. The male and female spinners then mate and the male spinner, his reproductive cycle over, dies. The female spinner, however, lays her eggs underwater as described and so the life cycle continues before she in turn dies. At almost all these stages in its life cycle the aquatic fly provides an essential and desirable source of food for trout; furthermore at each stage, nymph, dun, spinner, male or female, can be imitated successfully, and such artificial imitations may catch fish if properly presented at the right place and time.

The Duns
Perhaps the commonest group of aquatic flies to be found hatching on the water during the fishing season are the duns, which are much copied as artificial flies. Amongst the most common of the duns is the *Large Dark Olive*, which along with the *Iron Blue Dun* is usually to be found in the early part of the season, from April to May and again later in the season from September to October, particularly on rivers. Rather smaller and a little paler is the *Medium Olive*, found mostly from May through to September.

Commonest of all is the *Blue Winged Olive*, which may be found almost everywhere all through the season and is particularly prevalent from the end of June until August. It is a favourite for the evening rise.

The Trichoptera, Caddis, or Sedge Flies
Another important group of aquatic flies are the sedges. There are numerous variations, in size and colouring, but most tend to be found during the evening. These flies, in their various stages, are also favourite feed for the trout. There are three stages after the eggs are dropped in the water; the eggs attach themselves to reeds or stones and from them the larvae, or caddis emerge; then they form an outer case and live on minute algae and animal matter. Around a year later the pupa hatches from the caddis and swims to the surface where it emerges as a sedge fly.

The Stonefly
The stonefly is only found in the colder climate from Yorkshire northwards. The wingless stonefly larvae, or creeper, is what the trout prefer and can prove a most attractive bait. Stoneflies, which may grow up to half an inch in length, are also often a useful lure when worked across fast-moving water.

The March Brown
Another very well known large fly, which generally hatches in April and is mostly found hatching in rivers or fast-moving water, is the March Brown. The hatches do not generally last long but artificial March Browns are likely to be effective throughout the year. The nymph is flat and lives on the underside of stones, so that the fly is common throughout Scotland, Wales, Devon and northern England, but is rare on the chalk streams or silty southern rivers.

The Mayfly
Perhaps even better known, especially in the south of England, is the mayfly. Although it is less commonly found in Scotland, artificial imitations may still prove effective. The mayfly nymph is of the burrowing kind and is therefore commonly found in rivers with a silty, muddy

bed. The mayfly itself is the largest of the ephemeridae and generally hatches in the afternoons from the end of May to the middle of June, although in Ireland sometimes as late as August. It is, however, no longer as common as it used to be and in some areas now seems to have almost completely vanished.

The Diptera
The Black Gnat, although so-called, is neither a gnat nor black, but one of the diptera with a deep brown or olive body. It is frequently found in summer and autumn, flying in small clouds close to the surface of the water and readily taken by trout.

Worms, Grubs and Crustacea
Hungry trout may turn to feeding on grubs, beetles and similar insects which are blown into the water or fall from overhanging bushes, or branches. They will also eagerly feed on worms and small crustacea, shrimps and snails found in weed beds or in the silt of the river or lake bed.

Minnows and Smaller Fish
Trout, like most fish, as they increase in size will occasionally turn to eating minnows and smaller fish. As they grow larger and feed at greater depths this can become habitual so that eventually this food comprises all or most of their diet. In extreme cases they may develop pronounced cannibal habits and characteristics, and where there are char to be found in a lake or loch, they may take to feeding on them and living at a considerable depth as Ferox.

CHAPTER THREE

The Tackle

For the Beginner

On first entering any fishing tackle shop the average novice will simply be overcome by the displays of rods, reels, lines, nets, flies, fishing bags, coats, waders and similar paraphernalia all of which is displayed enticingly in front of him in a totally bewildering profusion. Some shops offer an absolutely amazing choice of tackle suitable for catching fish of all kinds, in almost every circumstance or place that can be imagined, from the Himalayas to the Seven Seas in every sort of weather known to man. There seems to be a rod for every purpose imaginable, built for giants and for dwarfs. Gleaming reels and fanciful flies assault the eye and the senses. It is easy for even the most cautious to end up buying tackle which merely remains in a cupboard and is never used.

The Bare Minimum

The answer is to start with the bare minimum required for the area where the fishing is to take place and to stick firmly to tackle for trout only. Tackle for marlin, for pike or for salmon, is strictly outside present requirements and, at a stroke, half the tackle in the shop may be seen as of no interest. Even so it is as well, if possible, to have an experienced trout angler as a guide to essentials. Otherwise it will be necessary to explain to the salesman what is required and rely on his advice. The average sensible tackle shop salesman, faced with a complete beginner, knows that if he provides him with the essentials required, and gives him good advice, he will have a grateful client returning to him regularly both for further advice and to boast of his successes and mourn his failures over the years ahead. There is always a tendency to buy too much, but that is one of the first pitfalls of fishing and one into which every angler is likely to fall not just once but many times.

The Essentials for Fly Fishing
The Fly Rod
The average fly rod is designed with a certain degree of bend, which is known as the 'action'. Some rods have a very whippy tip, but are otherwise rather stiff, while other rods bend more readily from the tip to the middle. Yet other rods may be found which bend right through from the butt to the tip, which is known as butt action. To start with it is likely that the beginner will find it easier to cast with a rod having a fairly stiff action, although a rod with a slow butt action tends to make for longer casting.

The Perfect Fly Rod
In theory the perfect action for a fly casting rod should be obtained from a rod built in one piece; and such rods are obtainable, although they have the obvious disadvantage that they are difficult to transport from one place to another. For ease of transport most fly rods are made in two, three, or more jointed sections and are usually carried in a canvas or metal rod case for convenience and protection.

The Rod Yesterday
The material from which a rod is made has varied over the years. The old favourite used to be greenheart, but greenheart rods, like hickory golf clubs, are now collector's items. The same, to a large extent, is true of split-cane rods, made, as the name implies, from jointed pieces of split cane bound together to provide a balanced rod. These were followed by glass fibre rods, which are virtually obsolete today, although still used in some spinning rods. Such rods are light and tough, well able to withstand hard use.

The Rod Today
The lightest and most popular material for rod making nowadays, however, is graphite, or carbon fibre. Rods made of carbon fibre or boron fibre are exceptionally light and easy to cast and this is the standard material in use at present. One of the few objections to carbon fibre rods is that in exceptional cases, when under strain and subjected to a blow, they have been known to disintegrate,

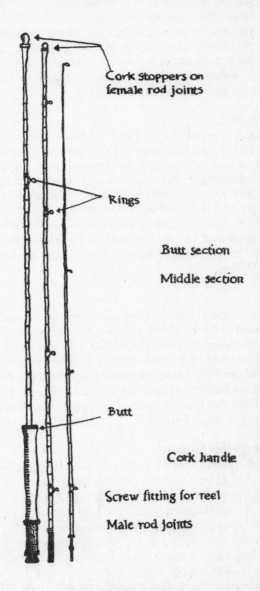

Cork stoppers on
female rod joints

Rings

Butt section

Middle section

Butt

Cork handle

Screw fitting for reel

Male rod joints

PARTS OF A FISHING ROD

as for instance when a fish is being played and the rod is under stress and a branch or similar object strikes the rod. Such rods are, however, generally sturdy under normal conditions. One other point is that graphite, or carbon fibre, is an excellent conductor of electricity so that fishing in a thunderstorm is inadvisable, but any wet rod with metal rings presents a similar hazard.

The Length
The length is a matter for the individual, to some extent. There used to be a tendency for shorter and shorter rods to be used, down to around 8 feet or even less, but now that such a lightweight material is available the tendency has been to turn to longer rods of 9 feet or more once again. The advantage of a long rod is that it can do almost everything a shorter rod can do, but the reverse is not equally true. A short rod cannot be used to cast as far and carry as much line. The most popular length is probably between 9 1/2 and 10 1/2 feet.

The Fly Reel
There are a great many different types of fly reel on the market and at first sight the choice may seem bewildering. The major point to look for is that the reel suits the rod that has been bought. The weight and balance of the two combined are very important and they should be tried out together to ensure that they match each other well. The reel should hold the line as well as sufficient backing to allow for playing a large fish.

Interchangeable Spools
It is a good plan to buy a reel with interchangeable spools so that, should you feel the need to do so, you can change the weight or type of line being used without undue trouble. An alternative is to buy two identical reels with different types of line so that should one break, or jam irretrievably, the other can be brought into play and thus avoid losing a day's sport. To have some such mishap arise resulting in the loss of a fish is bad enough; but when it means abandoning a day's sport, usually just when the fish are beginning to rise, it can be a disaster.

The Line Weight

The weight of the line is of considerable importance in the matter of casting. The correct weight of line for the rod will result in a much longer line being cast. Most rod manufacturers tend to specify the ideal line weight, which is likely to be stamped on the butt. If the line is too light the angler will find it difficult, if not impossible to cast effectively, especially against any sort of wind. On the other hand using a line that is too heavy can damage the rod itself.

Buoyancy

There are many types of line available today but the majority are made from a tough plaited Terylene inner core covered with a smooth plastic coating. By incorporating minute air bubbles in the plastic a degree of buoyancy can be added to the line, varying as desired, so that either the entire line remains floating, or only the tip of the line sinks, or the entire line sinks slowly; or, if preferred, so that the entire line sinks quickly. Lines of the latter kind are made from a high density material to ensure fast and deep sinking. Whether a line is required to sink or float depends on the type of fishing involved. When fishing with a dry fly in clear water it may be desirable to have a line floating on top of the water, whereas in a loch or reservoir it might be desirable to fish deep and have a line which sinks immediately on landing on the water.

Floating Lines

These can be obtained in various colours, brown, green and white. The theory is that the white line reflects light and casts a shadow, which is broken up and less easily seen. A ripple on the water and dappled light and shadow probably has a similar effect. It is largely a matter for personal preference. I prefer green because it seems to me more natural and to blend better with most backgrounds, but brown and white seem to work just as well.

Sinking Lines

There are several varieties on the market with different speeds of sinking. Too fast a sinking line is probably a nuisance since in shallower waters it will constantly be snagging the bottom, and few people can afford several different sinking lines and reels to go with them. One ordinary fast-sinking line is probably enough unless you intend to fish very deep indeed, i.e. over 9 feet.

Tapered Lines
Double Taper
In addition to floating or sinking lines it is possible to have lines of varied thickness. For example it is possible to buy what is termed a double-taper line which has a gentle taper towards each end and is thickest in the centre. This permits a more delicate presentation of the nylon cast, or leader, to which the fly or flies are attached. Then, as one end wears out the line can be rewound on the.reel with the reverse end in use thus allowing it to be used again from the other end. The double taper line is generally used on rivers rather than on still water.

Forward Taper
The double taper line is useful, especially for novices, but does not make for long casting. For lengthy casting, especially into a wind the forward taper line is specially designed. As the name implies the forward taper line is thicker at the end than in the middle. The aim is to supply weight where it is desired for longer casting, although naturally enough this is achieved at the expense of delicacy of presentation. Such lines are generally used mostly on large reservoirs or lakes, where it is desired to cast an especially long line. They are not something the novice need bother about initially.

Shooting Head Cast
For extra long casting, especially in lakes and reservoirs, the above technique is sometimes enhanced by the use of a specially designed shooting head cast. This consists merely of some 10 yards or so of line attached to a nylon backing on the reel. The much heavier weight of the line, compared with the lighter nylon backing, shoots the nylon with it allowing for very lengthy casts, but this is once again certainly not a method to be attempted by beginners.

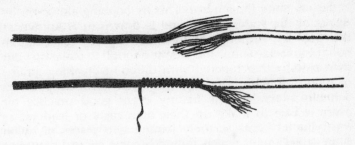

SPLICING THE LINE

Backing

Depending on the size of the reel anything from 10–25 yards of Terylene line may initially be wound on to the drum of the reel to provide 'backing' for the proper line, as a safeguard in case a large trout strips all the normal line off the reel while being played. The two lines must, of course, be carefully spliced together to permit the join to slide easily through the rings of the rod. When fishing in open spaces, such as lochs or reservoirs, more backing is likely to be required than when fishing in rivers or more restricted areas, but in any event the amount of backing available will, of necessity, be limited by the size of the reel.

The Cast, or Leader

Tied to the end of the line itself it is necessary to have a fine nylon cast, or leader, some 10 or more feet long, to which the fly, or flies, are attached. Such casts may be bought ready made from any tackle shop and may either be a tapered cast, which is naturally more expensive, or of the same width throughout its length. It may have one or more 'droppers' attached to it at intervals of around 3 feet or so from the end.

The Droppers

Artificial flies are attached to the end of the nylon cast and to the droppers for wet fly fishing. If two droppers are used this provides a tail fly at the end fished below the surface and the fly on the first dropper also just below the surface, while the fly on the dropper nearest the rod is drawn along the surface. This fly bobbing along on the ripple of the water as the line is drawn in is known as the 'bob' fly. Although as indicated tapered casts can be bought in tackle shops it is simple enough to make up your own casts, either tapered with different breaking strains of nylon, or with one length of nylon with droppers at suitable intervals. It is in any event good practice for every novice to make up their own casts or leaders, as the tying of knots securely joining two pieces of nylon is an achievement which should become second nature to every angler. It is not difficult and the sooner it is learned the better. (See p.45)

Nylon

It is important to realise that monofilament nylon deteriorates quite quickly with age and use. At the end of each season it is important to get rid of any nylon casts or lines, because keeping them is a false economy. While they may appear perfectly sound to the untrained eye, the probability is that they will snap the first time you are into a trout, and there is nothing more annoying than losing what will undoubtedly seem the finest fish of the day through personal stupidity of this nature.

Flies and Fly Boxes

Artificial flies are to be had in almost every imaginable size and colour. Suggestions as to the most suitable choice for different occasions will come later. The fly box in which the flies are kept, however, is an essential item of equipment and must be included here. Basically any container may be used for flies, from an old tobacco tin to tailor-made gleaming contraptions with clips, foam, felt, or magnets to hold the flies in place, or those with special compartments for the flies and a perspex top through which they may be seen. At a pinch, as indicated, almost anything will do to hold flies, but I prefer a plastic top and magnetic holders, as there is a danger of clips damaging the barbs of flies and hence losing a fish at a vital moment. Hooks can also become rusty if kept in wet foam or felt. It is largely a matter of individual preference, but keeping all the flies jumbled together in a tin is not really practical as they are often not at all easy to disentangle and may readily become damaged.

The Net

Numerous patent collapsible landing nets are available with telescopic handles and clips for fastening to belts, and most of them are useful and convenient to use. The larger they are the better, since this makes netting the fish easier and more certain. It is also decidedly preferable to use one without large knots in evidence as these may damage the scales of a fish which would otherwise be better returned to the water. The old plain round net which screws into a wooden handle, and which can be used as a wading staff and carried by a cord round the shoulders when not in use, is totally reliable, if possibly a little more awkward to carry. It cannot fail to open at a tricky moment, and there is

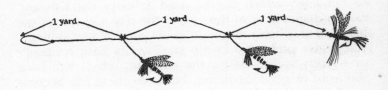

THE THREE-FLY CAST
from left BOB, DROPPER, TAIL

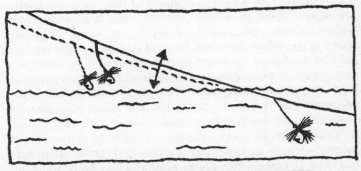

THE ACTION OF THE 'BOB' FLY ON THE WATER

no danger of a telescopic handle jamming. It only requires one fish to be lost in such a way to make the angler swear never to use a telescopic folding net again. On the other hand most people will continue to do so because of their undoubted convenience. There is, nevertheless, still a lot to be said in favour of the old reliable round net.

Fishing Bag

What sort of fishing bag, if any, an angler has is entirely up to the individual. There are considerable numbers and varieties of fishing bags on the market, but one with an adjustable strap to sling over the shoulder is usually preferable. A number of special pockets for items such as spare reels, fly box and casts is a good idea to prevent these all being jumbled together and possibly damaged. Most specially designed fishing bags contain a waterproof pocket for the catch, but even if this has a detachable and washable lining it is advisable to take carrier bag, or bin liner, which can be used to carry the fish and can be disposed of at the end of the day. Otherwise the bag will inevitably begin to smell after a few outings. Altogether preferable is the small raffia bass container or wicker creel made for the purpose, which will keep the trout in good condition, but even these can become smelly after a while.

Wellingtons versus Thigh Waders

Most anglers will wish to include a pair of good water-proof wellingtons in their equipment, for there are many occasions, even in a boat, when wet feet will result without them. When fishing from the bank there are many times when they will be useful. Good thigh waders may be preferred by some on the grounds that there are undoubtedly occasions when wading over knee deep is helpful and when they may make all the difference to the enjoyment of the day's sport. Thigh waders with heavily studded soles are the best kind to buy. Although bulky to carry they are easy enough to walk in and provide protection against brambles, nettles and similar bankside hazards. If you do buy them remember to hang them up in a dry cupboard by a string round the feet, not by the straps fitted to hold them up to your trouser tops, or they will stretch when dry and soon crack and become useless.

Waders Chest High

The danger of wearing waders at all is that they encourage people to wade when it is not strictly necessary, in the hope of getting their line out ever further. More fish in fact are caught close in to the bank than most anglers appreciate. Chest waders I look on as downright dangerous. Not only do they encourage people to wade further than is strictly necessary, but in certain waters, especially fast-flowing rivers with rocky bottoms, they can be extremely dangerous. No one should use them without a stout wading staff and without knowing the water. In some rivers unexpected potholes or a dislodged stone may cause someone to slip and this is when chest waders may quickly start to fill. The danger in such circumstances is that while apparently standing squarely one moment, the next you are upside down with the waders filling rapidly. Air pockets then form in the feet of the waders which float to the surface while your head is forced under water. It is easy to panic in such circumstances and quite a few people have drowned in this way. There is a move to introduce legislation making it compulsory for anglers to wear some form of lifejacket or buoyancy aid and especially when wading, or fishing from a boat, or even from a steep bank, this makes good sense.

A Priest

Every angler should carry a priest which is in effect a small weighted cudgel for killing a fish humanely and quickly by a sharp tap behind the gills at the base of the head. Leaving the wretched fish to expire in the bottom of the boat or flapping helplessly on the bank, gasping out its life, is sheer cruelty. Relying on any available stone or stick is simply not good enough, and is seldom very effective.

Clothing and Other Minor Essentials

One of the first essentials is to have a full set of wind and waterproof clothing. A useful standby is to wear a showerproof jacket and carry a lightweight windproof and waterproof overjacket rolled up in the fishing bag. It is advisable as well to have a lightweight pair of nylon over-trousers, which can also be readily carried in the fishing bag. Special waterproof over-waistcoats designed for anglers can also be useful, with pockets for various minor essentials such as fly boxes, knives and so on.

Inflatable Buoyancy Pack

An inflatable buoyancy pack is an item well worth carrying in a pocket at all times when fishing, whether in a boat, or wading, or fishing from the bank. These small but lifesaving items are now readily obtainable. They are not expensive and they could save your life.

Ancillaries

Wherever possible certain other minor items should always be to hand, whether in a pocket or in the fishing bag and conveniently available:

A pair of Polaroid spectacles, which cut out glare from the water and can on occasions help you to see trout beneath the surface more clearly.

A sharp knife, is an essential, preferably one designed especially for anglers with attachments such as a disgorger for removing hooks from a fish's throat, a file for sharpening barbs, or removing them from hooks (a pair of pliers also do the job effectively), and a pair of scissors for cutting nylon or line. The latter can save tooth wear since strong nylon can easily chip the teeth when endeavouring to bite it.

Line floatant to apply to line or fly to keep them afloat should be kept to hand in a convenient pocket ready for use whenever necessary.

A stomach spoon. A marrow spoon was used by the famous chalk stream fly fisher G.E.M. Skues, and special spoons are available today in most tackle shops. Thrusting this down the trout's throat into the stomach and turning it before slowly extracting it will remove the stomach contents. If these are then floated off in a small bowl of water it is possible to tell what the trout are mainly feeding on and match the flies, if you wish to do so. This is, however, not something the beginner need worry about initially.

A good waterproof and windproof hat is a decided asset. One with peaks which can be pulled down to keep the ears warm and which will also keep the neck dry is a boon. There are few designs to beat the Sherlock Holmes headgear, with flaps tied on top when not in use. The fur-lined twin peaked cap used by camouflaged troops in arctic conditions is also a useful form of headgear. Some form of 'fore-and-after' headgear, protecting both face and neck, is certainly a great advantage in wet or snowy conditions.

Useful Items to Carry

Anti-midge cream, or spray is almost an essential in some areas, particularly the highlands of Scotland.

Spare leaders, already made up on cast carriers, are always worth having, since it is not unknown for the most expert of anglers to get a cast in a tangle occasionally. Also this facilitates changing flies if you have varied casts ready to hand.

A creel or bass, to hold the fish and keep them fresh is really much better than a plastic bag, but even they tend to get smelly unless treated with care.

A torch is always worth having in a pocket in case darkness catches you still flogging the water, and can save you leaving some vital and expensive item of equipment behind on the river bank.

The Essentials for Spinning
The Spinning Rod

The rod for spinning, as opposed to a fly rod, is much stiffer and shorter, with far less whip. The aim of spinning is to cast the bait so that it flies freely a considerable distance before being reeled back to the angler. The bait may be weighted to carry further and the rod must be strong enough to withstand considerable pressures in such casting. As with fly rods the materials from which the rod is made may vary in the same way, but in this case strength as well as lightness are the important elements.

The Fixed Spool Reel

A fixed spool reel used for bait casting and spinning is very different from a fly casting reel. The reel, as indicated by the name, is fixed and the line leaves it under the impetus of the cast to be retrieved by a mechanical device and re-threaded on the spool as it is reeled in. There are numerous different makers of fixed spool reels, but basically they all work on the same principle. The line is released at the moment of casting and is retrieved by reeling in steadily, thus causing the bait, or minnow, to travel through the water in an enticing manner.

Interchangeable Spools

As in the case of fly reels it is a good idea to have interchangeable spools available so that if need be they can quickly be changed. One reason for this may be that it is felt a stronger line may be required, with a greater breaking strain, for unlike fly lines, fixed spool lines are made of nylon with various breaking strains. This material, like that of the fly fisher's cast, can readily get tangled in a

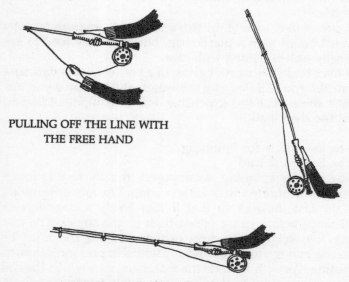

PULLING OFF THE LINE WITH
THE FREE HAND

THE CORRECT WAY TO HOLD THE ROD

way which may be very difficult to rectify. In the event of a mistake in casting with a fixed spool reel a bird's nest of nylon can sometimes result, and having a spare reel available may be the simplest solution for the beginner. The bird's nest can then be put away to sort out at leisure and the day's sport is not spoiled.

Spinning Baits, Swivels and Weights

As with artificial flies the question of baits, swivels and weights will be largely dealt with later. Here it is only necessary to say that ball-bearing swivels are an essential and should be used as a matter of course regardless of the bait. There are various kinds of zinc-alloy weights (lead is now illegal), but it is also desirable to add an anti-kink vane, weighted or unweighted, which is fitted directly to the line above the swivel and together with it prevents the monofilament line from very soon becoming irretrievably twisted and useless.

A Warning

It is essential always to ensure that you do not leave any pieces of nylon lying around in which unwary birds or beast may become entangled. Each year there are unfortunately many cases of wretched creatures becoming entangled in discarded nylon and dying an unpleasant death as a result. Discarding any rubbish such as used beer cans is also not only unsightly but likely to cause more work for someone else, and may even end up with anglers being banned from the area in question.

CHAPTER FOUR

Initial Dry Practice and Preparation

Where to Start
It is undoubtedly best for the complete novice to keep his tackle to a minimum, rather than being lured into buying several rods and reels and numerous flies before he starts. Choosing neither a very short rod nor a very long one, a 9 or 9 1/2 foot rod will probably fulfill all requirements until the fishing technique is learned; a matching reel and line and a cast of fairly stout proportions, say a 6 lb breaking strain, are probably quite sufficient. It is necessary, however, before starting to fish to learn certain very simple knots which have to be used on every occasion.

The Knots
The Figure-of-Eight
The first of these is the figure-of-eight knot used for the purpose of joining the thinner nylon cast, or leader, to the line itself. As the illustration opposite shows this could hardly be simpler and soon becomes second nature.

The Turle
This is another simple knot used to hold the fly firmly in place on the end of the nylon cast or to the dropper. Whenever dry fly fishing or nymphing, the fly or nymph should be attached directly to the cast with a turle knot. This is absolutely essential and again very simple to learn.

The Full Blood Knot
Perhaps the simplest of all knots this is used to join two pieces of nylon and can also be used, if required, to form a dropper for a fly in a wet fly cast. A very practical knot in frequent use.

a)  b)

THE FULL BLOOD KNOT, FOR JOINING NYLON

**THE TURLE KNOT,
FOR TYING FLY TO CAST**

**THE FIGURE-OF-EIGHT KNOT,
FOR JOINING LINE TO CAST**

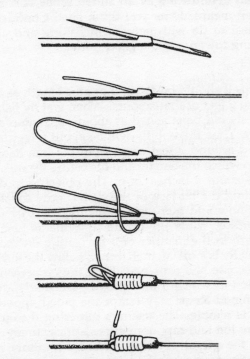

THE NEEDLE KNOT, FOR ATTACHING A LEADER

The Needle Knot

Slightly trickier although still simple enough, but in any event less commonly used, is the needle knot for joining a tapered leader to the line so that the join does not stick in the rod rings and allows for longer casting. This is not one that the beginner need bother about, but may come in useful later. Some people use instant glue in addition here.

Variants

Some people inevitably prefer to use their own knots and there are those who prefer, for instance, to use a double turle, rather as there are people who prefer to wear belts with braces on their trousers. Instant glue can also be used instead of, or in addition to, some knots but tends to become unstuck after immersion in water. If such precautions give the angler an added sense of confidence then by all means do as you think best. Confidence has a great deal to do with success in fishing and anything contributing towards it is a good thing.

The Cast

The cast itself should be about the same length as the rod, say around 9 feet or thereabouts. When wet fly fishing the droppers should be attached at about yard intervals from the tail fly. Thus the bob fly will be about 6 feet from the tail fly and around 3 feet or so from the line itself. Each dropper to which the bob fly and the centre fly are attached should be about 3 inches long. The object is to drift the bob fly along the surface of the water, only touching on the water now and then, in the manner of a fly dancing on the surface, while the centre fly remains just on the surface film, in the manner of a fly resting on the water, and the tail fly is sunk an inch or two below the surface, as if it has become half drowned. Each thus represents a fly in a position in which it may prove particularly attractive to a feeding trout, or may tempt the jaded appetite of a trout that is resting. The use of a glittering fly, such as a Butcher, on the tail, may sometimes appear to an unwary trout like the glitter of some intrusive minnow chasing the centre fly or the bob and can thus prove effective in drawing attention to them, even if not actually catching a fish itself. For the initial dry casting practice no flies are required, although a single fly with neither barb nor hook may be attached to the cast to simulate the real thing and add a realistic touch of weight.

Initial Dry Casting Practice
The Back Cast
It is undoubtedly advisable to practise casting first on dry land. For dry casting a nylon cast may be attached to the line but with no flies, or at best only a hookless fly for a start. The technique of casting on a lawn is exactly the same as casting on water and it does not take long to master it. The services of an experienced angler are valuable, but it can be done alone. While it is not advisable to start practicing on a very windy day it is well worth starting with the wind behind so that it helps to send the cast forward. The classic teaching method is to regard oneself as standing on the right hand of a large vertical clock face. The rod is held at 3 o'clock with the amount of line it is proposed to cast, say about 3 or 4 yards, already pulled off the reel by hand and lying on the lawn below the rod tip. With the forearm straight and the elbow held into the body the rod is raised firmly and steadily upwards and backwards to 12 o'clock. When the thumb and the butt of the rod are almost vertical and coming nearly level with the eyes the line should all have passed overhead. This is known as the backcast. The important thing is to let the rod itself do the bulk of the work. Regardless of whether the angler is casting from a boat, or from the bank, or wading, the mechanics of casting are exactly the same. The secret of success is to make a very slight pause at the vertical, or near 12 o'clock position, to allow the line to overtake the movement of the rod and achieve a near horizontal straight line behind the angler's shoulder. At this stage it is the whip, or bend, of the tip of the rod which does the main work, carrying the line backwards.

The Forward Cast
After a brief and barely perceptible pause at the top of the backcast the rod is brought forward with equal steadiness

and firmness to around the 2 o'clock position. Once again it is the bend of the rod tip, this time in the opposite direction, which does all the work. The line should then travel forward in a straight line from the rod tip to the full extent available. It is important to avoid as far as possible making any jerky movements of the arm, or of the shoulder, or bending the wrist, or the result will be whiplash effect which very frequently causes the tail fly and sometimes even the other flies as well, to be whipped off the line (hence the point of having a hookless fly attached). After a few initial faults the average beginner will soon start to cast confidently and accurately on dry land, directing the line where he wants it to go, and it will be found there is in fact little or no difference between casting on dry land or over water.

Practice at a Target
Initially it is as well to start by practicing such dry casting, preferably on a lawn, or wide expanse of flat ground, with no obstacles such as trees or bushes in the area. It is a good idea to lay a target on the ground to aim at so that one can begin to measure one's accuracy. Something about the size of the lid of a shoe box at a distance of around 25 or 30 feet would be suitable. The secret of success is that very slight pause in the vertical or near 12 o'clock position to allow the line to overcome the movement of the rod and achieve a nearly horizontal straight line behind the angler's shoulder, before gently moving the arm and the rod in a straight line forward once more. The whip, or bend in the rod tip, should be allowed to tackle the weight of the line and carry it fully out backwards and then cast it straight forward at the aiming point.

Casting Variations
By simply practicing steadily on grass or in an open space, the average person will soon become proficient enough at simple casting in this way. It is advisable to continue until it becomes a natural and automatic habit. After a surprisingly short time most people will be pleased to find they are even beginning to achieve a fair degree of

accuracy. It may then be advisable to start casting across the wind and even into the wind to learn to overcome these handicaps.

False Casting and Shooting Line

When casting the line initially the novice will simply cast the amount of line released from the reel. In the next step the left hand may be used to strip a yard or two more line off the reel. This can be easily held in the left hand in a loose coil. In this way the beginner can then start to practice increasing the amount of line cast. This is done by casting forward and then, instead of allowing the line to settle, returning to the near vertical position and casting again. This is known as false casting and on the second forward cast it is possible to release the line held loosely in the left hand to gain extra distance. This is known as 'shooting the line'. In this way it should soon be a simple matter to add as much as 2 or 3 yards or more to the cast without any real additional effort. False casting in this way can also be used as an aid to accuracy in casting the line exactly where it is required to land it. By shooting the line in this way the beginner will soon find it possible to add materially to the amount of line being cast until the maximum amount that can be readily controlled is being cast. A warning footnote should be added to the effect that it is easy enough to get carried away with the success of this method until it is overdone. If the novice attempts to cast more line than the combination of rod length and weight of line will allow, the result will be an unseemly tangle of line around the would-be angler along with a total failure of the cast. The novice should then restrict the length of the cast accordingly.

Backhand Casting

Backhand casting, very similar to the action required in a backhand tennis, squash, or badminton shot, is also mastered easily enough. It is in effect exactly the same action as the forward cast, allowing the rod tip to do the bulk of the work in the near vertical position. This form of casting is essential when fishing from a boat and enables the angler to cast comfortably in the stern end of a boat when his companion is casting in the forepart, thus ensuring that their lines do not cross each other and become entangled. Without this precaution it is only too easy for this to happen and it can cause considerable trouble disentangling them in the close confines of a boat. The backhand cast can also often be used to good effect to avoid becoming entangled with awkwardly placed bushes or trees on the riverbank. It can also be very useful when casting in a cross wind.

Underhand or Sideways Casting

A further refinement is underhand or sideways casting, very much in the same form as a forehand or backhand stroke at tennis, although here the wrist may be rotated as the cast is made with a twisting and flicking movement. This again can be used to very good effect when it is necessary to stay fairly close to the water to avoid obstructions such as tree branches or bushes overhanging the bank and is well worth practicing. For the early stages these are sufficient to cover most of the angler's requirements and are all that need be practised.

The Initial Faults

The usual faults the novice is likely to make are in going too far back on the backcast or conversely going too far forward with the forward cast, or very often in failing to allow sufficient pause at the top of the backcast. Going too far back with the backcast is usually due to snatching the line too fast and eagerly backwards, and may result in catching the cast on the ground behind the angler, or, in reality, splashing in the water or catching the bank behind. Similarly, allowing the rod tip to go too far forward may result in the line splashing into the water in front. Both will result in untidy, ineffectual casting, while failing to allow sufficient pause on the backcast will very often result in the flies being flicked off the cast by the resultant whiplash effect. It is essential to learn to make a steady measured backcast and follow through with a straight cast forward. While all novices inevitably differ in natural ability it should not take long to learn to cast efficiently with a fly rod.

Wrist Support

The young, and those with weak wrists, tend to find that after casting for a while their wrist is weakening, with the result that they cease to control the rod properly and their casting suffers. Almost any angler may begin to feel

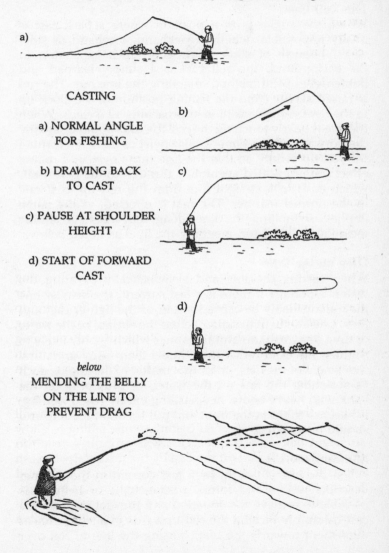

CASTING

a) NORMAL ANGLE
   FOR FISHING

b) DRAWING BACK
   TO CAST

c) PAUSE AT SHOULDER
   HEIGHT

d) START OF FORWARD
   CAST

below
MENDING THE BELLY
ON THE LINE TO
PREVENT DRAG

his wrist tiring after a long day of casting. A simple and effective remedy is merely to turn the rod round so that the reel is against the underside of the wrist and providing a natural and effective support.

The Roll Cast
Where the angler is in a position where a back cast is totally impossible, whether backhand, forehand or side-ways, because of some obstruction such as bushes in the background, the roll cast is a simply learned and immensely useful method of getting the line out. The rod is raised slowly from the fishing position of 3 o'clock up to the near vertical position approaching 12 o'clock. When the line is nearly touching the reel the rod should be swiftly cast forward with a semi-circular twist of the wrist turning the rod tip swiftly so that the line turns over in a rolling effect communicated eventually through to the cast itself, which ends in a straight line from the rod tip as if cast in the normal manner. The cast is effected, as the name implies, by rolling the line along the water. A similar technique is used for 'mending the line' as noted below.

Drag on the Line
When casting the line and systematically covering the water, especially if there is a fast current, the heavier line may unavoidably be carried ahead of the lighter cast and flies, causing them to skitter across the surface of the water or drag in a most unnatural manner which is only likely to frighten the trout rather than attract them. Any unnatural movement of the flies, or for that matter of the angler, such as splashing the line on the water, or thumping on the bank with heavy boots, or splashing loudly when wading, is likely to frighten the trout and put them off feeding and should be avoided.

Mending the Line
When the line is caught by a fast current in the manner described above and forms a semi-circle, or belly, it is possible to retrieve the situation and prevent drag on the cast by simply flicking the rod upwards in a semi-circular movement towards the cast, causing the line to roll over

and reverse the bellying action. In very fast currents it may sometimes be necessary to perform this action several times to allow the cast to move naturally without drag. The process, a simple one once learned, is known descriptively as 'mending the line'. This is a technique very similar to roll casting (and just as easily mastered) which can prove invaluable at times. It is especially useful when fishing across a river or stream. Then the bulk of the line is often in the fast-moving central current but the flies are in the comparatively much slower moving shallow waters on the far side, close beneath the far bank, where trout are often to be found. Mending the line can easily enough be practiced on dry land, but, like the roll cast, in fact works much more readily on the water since on land the line is liable to move less easily than it does on the water itself.

Spinning

For spinning, as has been indicated, a shorter and stiffer rod is generally required; also, a fixed spool reel with a slipping clutch is used, with nylon line of varying breaking strength. A bait, or lure, such as a minnow, which may or may not rotate, or spin, rather than flies, is attached to the end of of the nylon line, with or without an added lead weight to allow it to be cast further.

The Cast

The cast itself may be overhand, backhand, forehand, sideways and underhand and is more akin to a flick than the smooth backward and forward cast used in fly fishing. Before starting the cast the line is released from its winding mechanism and then is held firmly against the rod itself with the forefinger of the casting hand. The rod is then gently taken back to the start of the casting position and is swung forward smartly. With the start of the forward movement the forefinger releases the line allowing the weighted lure, or bait, to fly forward to achieve the maximum trajectory and distance.

The Second Stage

As soon as the bait, or lure, is seen to land on the water the winding-in process should start in order to prevent what is known as an over-run on the reel. Especially when a miscast has occurred as a result of mistiming the release of the line, it sometimes happens that too much line is stripped off the spool allowing the nylon line to form a massive tangle or 'bird's nest'. This usually takes a considerable time to disentangle and is not conducive to good temper. Although such mistakes may happen occasionally to start with, it fortunately does not take long to become accustomed to the fixed spool reel method of both casting and spinning so that such accidents become increasingly rare.

Practice Casting
By using a weight on the end of the nylon line it is simple to practice various casts on any lawn or open space. The various methods of casting, overhand, backhand, sideways, and underhand should all be practiced and the moment the weight lands the winding-in process should begin automatically. It is the somewhat mechanical nature of this form of fishing which many people find rather inhibiting, but it should be possible to cast considerable distances with a fair degree of accuracy after a certain amount of practice. Once confidence is established the time comes to try the real thing.

Prior Preparations
It is always advisable to check all the tackle before leaving home to ensure that nothing vital, such as the rod, net, or boots is left behind. It is imperative in this context not to forget the vitally important fishing permit, rod licence or similar authorisation without which it may be necessary to pay twice over or not be allowed to fish at all. Foul weather clothing and suitable supplies of food and drink are also important aids to ensuring a satisfactory day, although not as all-important as tackle and permit. At a pinch it is possible to get wet or go hungry and thirsty and still have a first rate day, but with sensible preparation this should not be necessary. It is therefore always worth making a final check before leaving.

Rod Carriage

The rod itself may be set up in advance and transported on special fittings on the car roof, with the butt foremost as it should always be carried. There are a variety of such fittings but whatever kind is used it is always worth double checking them before starting off since if they have come loose, or are showing signs of wear, the rod is bound to suffer and the day can be ruined as a result. In such cases the rod is usually set up with reel, line and cast in position, but, although some people do not seem to mind driving miles with the rod carried in this way, I am never very happy about carrying it very far in such circumstances.

The Safest Method

To my mind the best and safest method of transporting the rod for any considerable distance is in the rod case inside the car. Although the rod is comparatively safe outside, there is always bound to be a danger of something happening to it in such an exposed position. An overhanging banch, or some obstruction on the road, may catch and damage it. It is also an open invitation to thieves if the car is parked anywhere; at the very least the rod will be exposed to the elements and may end up soaking wet. While this may not really matter very much it is not likely to do the reel much good. The reel, with backing already spliced to the line, with spare spool, or reel, in reserve, should already have been mounted on the rod. The same should be true of a cast, with spare casts and suitable change of flies in reserve ready for use if required.

The Final Check

The rest of the tackle: net, fishing bag (containing spare flies, casts, reels, clothing, permits and so on), should be ready but should still be double checked before leaving. It is unfortunately one of the immutable laws of fishing that whenever anything is left behind it is inevitably the one thing that was most required and without which the day is irretrievably ruined.

Arriving at the Water

If the rod has been carried on top of the car and is ready for use then it is merely a question of checking it over. If, however, it has been carried inside in the rod case the first thing is to ensure that it is set up and the reel attached. The line is then inserted through the rod rings and the leader attached. Care should always be taken in this process too. It is always annoying to find that a ring has been overlooked after the leader is attached and the whole process has to be repeated.

Care of The Rod

Another danger which can easily arise at this stage is leaning the set-up rod against the car with an open door. Should the rod slip into the hinges, or the door close with a sudden gust of wind this can very readily result in the rod snapping. Leaving the rod lying on the ground is another dangerous habit as many rods have been trodden on and broken in this way. Care should always be taken at this stage of the proceedings. Haste to get on the water can often lead to disastrous accidents.

The Preliminary Survey

If the angler has arrived at water that he, or she, has never fished before, a preliminary survey is advisable and enquiries will usually be well worthwhile. The manager of the water, if there is one present, will usually be very willing to help. In commercial fisheries it is in their interest for the anglers to catch fish and return as satisfied customers. In any event a glance at any fishing records available may be helpful, with details of likely flies and times of day, or even places, usually noted. Otherwise it is usually worth talking to any keeper, gillie, or other anglers who may be around and asking them for advice. In most cases this should result in some helpful tips on suitable flies and where to go. If no other advice is available it is a question of sizing up the water personally and deciding on the places that look most likely and heading for them. The time has now come to put theory into practice.

CHAPTER FIVE

Artificial Flies, Lures and Baits and Their Presentation

Flies and Nymphs

Artificial flies and nymphs as the name implies, are intended generally to be close imitations of the natural insects on which the trout are feeding and to deceive the fish accordingly. The general aim is to place the artificial fly or nymph above the fish and allow it to float down naturally in the hope that it will mistake the artificial offering for the real thing and swallow the hook. This may be done either by sinking the artificial imitation beneath the surface deliberately, as with a wet fly or nymph, or by floating it on the surface, as with a dry fly.

DIY

Dressing, or manufacturing, one's own flies is not as difficult as it might seem and with an inexpensive outfit even the complete novice can soon find this an enjoyable and rewarding occupation for evenings or non-fishing days. Apart from being an interesting pastime, all anglers should benefit from being able to tie their own flies. Apart from anything else, being able to match the fly that is being taken can sometimes mean the difference between catching or not catching fish.

Dry Flies

Artificial dry flies are usually tied with a hackle, or long thin feather wound round the body of the hook to resemble the wings, thorax and legs of the natural fly while at the same time aiding the buoyancy. These flies are tied with a cock bird's hackle, which, being firmer than the hen's, tends to float better. It is also an advantage that dry flies are most commonly used in clear, comparatively calm slow-flowing water, where trout can be seen feeding and rising. The aim is to cast the fly in such a position that it alights on the water with the minimum of disturbance and floats naturally over the circles left on the surface by the feeding trout, thus providing the best conditions for the artificial substitute to deceive the greedy fish. Since after a period of fishing the dry fly may become drowned, i.e. begin to sink, it is advisable to have a floatant in reserve with which to daub the fly and encourage it to remain floating.

Wet Flies and Nymphs

Wet flies and nymphs are generally tied from hen bird's hackles, which being softer, are more inclined to sink. Such wet flies are mostly used when there is a slight ripple on the water caused by wind, or in fast flowing water, where they are allowed to follow the natural current freely. The nymphs may be used in conditions suitable for either wet or dry fly where trout are seen feeding beneath the surface, causing a typical bulge on the water as they arch their backs. With both wet flies and nymphs it is worth twitching, or working them slightly at intervals as they float in the water to impart the impression of an insect struggling vainly as it is carried downwards in the current beneath the surface.

Lures

Those wet flies which are brightly tinselled, and resemble no known fly or aquatic creature, may more properly be termed lures and are generally worked across fast-flowing or rippling water beneath the surface in a series of short jerks, thus perhaps resembling some tiny water creature moving erratically through the current, or simply exciting the trout's curiosity. A similar method is generally employed with lures which are designed to resemble small creatures such as minnows, worms, or crustacea such as freshwater shrimps. The vast numbers of brightly coloured wet flies and lures which fill the shelves and show cases of every tackle shop are quite remarkable, and the novice would do well to concentrate at the start on using a few well known artificial flies.

Hooks

There are various sizes and kinds of hook on which the artificial flies are tied and it is important to use the right size for the water. There is a standard scale of size as illustrated but makes vary. There are also different bends on the hooks, notably the round bend, usually best for trout, the Limerick bend, suitable for Sea trout, and the square bend, which some people prefer. Many hooks are bent off, or snecked, which may make them float unevenly in still water. Some people prefer double hooks which, being heavy, tend to sink deeper than a single hook, but they do have the snag that the second hook can sometimes act as a lever causing the trout to come free. The eye of the hook may be upturned, which is good for dry flies, or they may be downturned, or straight, but there is little to choose between the latter.

Speed of Retrieval
Much depends, of course, on whether the angler is fishing deep still water, or fast-flowing shallow river water, or something in between. In general, however, the speed of retrieval should try to imitate the natural insect and this can barely be too slow, with occasional hesitations when it is allowed to remain almost perfectly still. Yet there will often be occasions, especially when using one of the larger lures, when no matter how fast it is retrieved it seems a trout is determined to take it. This is especially the case with inexperienced, newly-introduced stock fish,

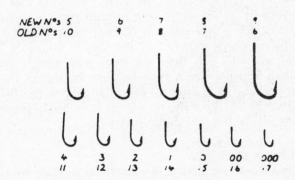

HOOK SIZES, OLD AND NEW

but it can also prove surprisingly effective on occasions on large and experienced wild Brown trout. There is clearly something about a large lure skittering across the surface of the water which arouses the interest and sometimes causes a determined take from a trout which one might have thought would have known better.

The Bait or Lure

As with flies, the variation in baits and lures is quite enormous and there is also a grey area where flies may almost be classified as lures and vice versa. A worm fly, for instance, or some Sea trout lures, used with fly rods, may well be regarded as more akin to spinning baits than flies, and indeed some may be used with a spinning rod to good effect. In general, however, the spinning bait, or lure is intended to resemble a small fishy meal swimming in the water rather than a fly which has landed on it or hatched in it. That about sums up the real difference between the two, although as indicated there are some which overlap and are more or less common to both categories.

Keeping the Fly on the Water

There are some anglers who consistently use the same fly or flies throughout the year and some of them have been known to catch fish consistently, but this may well have been due more to persistence or skill rather than the flies themselves. There is an old fisherman's saying that if you keep your fly on the water long enough you are eventually likely to catch a fish and it is certainly true that the man who fishes every moment of the day is far more likely to end up with fish than the man who simply sits on the bank and smokes a pipe because he thinks the fish are not taking. It is after all essential to give the fish the opportunity to take a fly, no matter how badly presented or how unlike the real thing it may be.

The Choice of Fly

This is something that it is almost impossible to advise on without knowing the local conditions. After a very few days of fishing everyone will have their own favourite flies which they swear by and which they are sure will catch fish. There are also certain places which fishermen tend to associate with certain flies. Similarly certain types of fly may be preferable in certain weather conditions. In overcast dull conditions, for instance, a dark fly may prove best, whereas in bright conditions the reverse may be the case, although on the face of it the opposite would seem to be more reasonable. Everyone will have their own preferences for one reason or another. As confidence is a large part of success in fishing, it is advisable always to fish with flies in which you have faith. At the same time, local knowledge can be a very useful thing and a glance at the fishing records, usually to be found in any fishing water, will generally include a note of which flies have been proving most effective. This will usually indicate the size of the fly used and of course the size varying with the different conditions can be all important. None of this will prevent certain people fishing consistently with flies which would appear to have little chance of success. The irritating thing, of course, is that sometimes they may catch a fish, in which case their belief in their fly becomes a certainty. Admittedly using certain favourites, such as March Brown, Peter Ross, Greenwell's Glory and Butcher throughout the year is something that has proved effective enough in practice over the years. They are flies which are likely to be found throughout most of the year on many waters. The size, however, must vary with the circumstances and conditions. The main thing is that the angler should present the flies consistently and cover the water thoroughly.

Selecting the Fly

To catch trout successfully it is always desirable to know what fly is most likely to be successful. There are several ways of doing this. One of the more scientific ways is to examine the stomach contents of the first trout caught. Slitting the stomach open with a sharp knife, or using a plastic tube, with or without a bulb, obtainable from most fishing tackle shops to take the stomach contents out is the first stage. Swilling these around in a shallow bowl of water reveals the flies on which the trout are feeding. It is

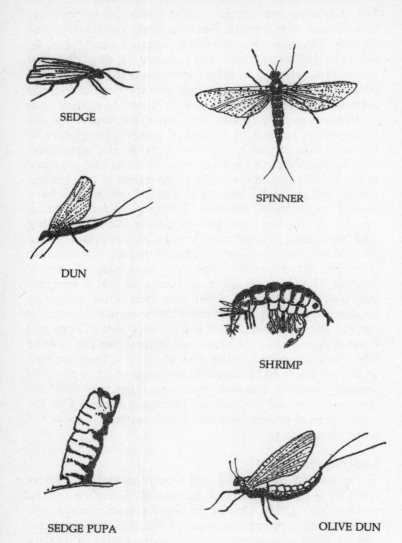

SEDGE

SPINNER

DUN

SHRIMP

SEDGE PUPA

OLIVE DUN

NATURAL FLIES AND LURES

ARTIFICIAL SEDGE

ARTIFICIAL SPINNER

ARTIFICIAL MIDGE PUPA

ARTIFICIAL SEDGE PUPA

ARTIFICIAL NYMPH

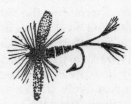

ARTIFICIAL DUN

GREENWELL'S GLORY
(REPRESENTING OLIVE DUN)

ARTIFICIAL SHRIMP

ARTIFICIAL FLIES AND LURES

first necessary, however, to catch a trout and this is not always easy. Nor is there always any guarantee that other trout are necessarily taking the same fly. A word with the water bailiff, or the nearest fishing tackle shop, or similar source of local knowledge, is usually a quicker, but not always certain, method of gaining the same information. Reference to the fishing record book will also usually inform the reader which flies are likely to prove most successful. Again this is not always a certain solution. Even with a perfectly matched artificial fly perfectly fished it is by no means certain the fish will be caught. It is one of the more infuriating and tantalising aspects of fishing that, despite every apparently correct action on the angler's part, the fish simply may not accept the fly.

Matching the Natural Fly

There can be few things more irritating for any angler than having trout rising freely on all sides, obviously feeding voraciously, and being unable to match the natural fly on which they are feeding. On these occasions, no matter how much you may cast over a rising fish, they will simply ignore your offering and continue to feed on the natural flies. Examining the flies on which they are feeding and providing as close an imitation as possible will sometimes have no effect at all. Conversely, once the rise is over, it may be that trout will then be caught on the artificial fly that had previously been refused. There is usually some comparatively simple solution, but at the time it is by no means always easy to find it. Such is the way of fishing; exasperating, maddening and when the correct solution is found extraordinarily satisfying.

Refusal to Accept the Fly

When the artificial fly or nymph has been carefully matched to the natural one on which the fish are feeding, there is still no guarantee that the fish will accept it. The solution may be plain enough; it may be that the fly, or nymph, is not being presented correctly. Perhaps the wet fly should be worked more vigorously, or more slowly, in the current. It may be that it is a little too large or a little too small.

Perhaps the hook is too prominent, or the nylon of the leader should be finer. It may be that the nymph is being fished too near the surface, or is moving too fast. Are the atmospheric conditions such that the fish are suddenly not interested in feeding? Is the water temperature colder than it was? These are the sort of questions the angler has to ask himself when all else seems to be correct but the fish are resolutely refusing to accept the artificial fly or nymph presented.

Recommended Checks

It sometimes happens that the fish appear to be interested in the fly but are not being hooked. This is generally referred to as 'taking short'. On such occasions it is always worth inspecting the fly, or flies, carefully. If a stone, or similar obstacle has been snagged it frequently happens that the barb is damaged or may even have snapped off completely. There are few things more irritating than losing fish through such elementary lack of care.

Size of Hook and Fly

Matching the artificial fly for size is of course highly important, and the hook size is the basis for this. For loch or reservoir fishing, depending on the area and the time of day, the hook size may vary from around No 12 to No 16. For evening fishing the size required is generally smaller. There is an old but apt saying that 'the brighter the sky the brighter the fly required', and the converse 'the darker the sky the darker the fly' is probably also true in most circumstances. The fact remains, however, that there are occasions when trout will refuse to rise to anything and equally there are occasions when against all expectations they will take a fly which seems totally unlikely to catch anything and which seems totally unsuited to the day or the circumstances.

Wet Flies

There are some anglers who consistently fish throughout the year with the same set of wet flies in all circumstances and who still catch fish. Nevertheless, it is desirable to try to match the flies to the occasion. An effective wet fly cast worth using in most conditions, however, might consist of a March Brown on the tail, reminiscent of a Blue Winged Olive dun, a Greenwell's Glory on the dropper, reminiscent of a Dark Olive dun, and a Silver Butcher on the bob dragging along the surface, glittering and flashing and likely to attract the attention and curiosity of a hungry trout. An Invicta on the bob, reminiscent of a hatching sedge and a White Chomper on the dropper, resembling a small pupa, might also prove successful in many circumstances. The variations are legion, but the general idea should be to try to match the food on which the trout are seen to be feeding, or on which they have been feeding recently.

Covering the Water Systematically
The trout, like most fish, has a comparatively limited field of vision and the angler can take advantage of this by casting upstream and allowing the fly to float naturally downstream until it reaches the stage where the fly is beginning to drag on the water at the end of the line and must then be retrieved for a further cast to be made. The initial casts should therefore be made in a direct line upstream from the angler covering the area nearest to him. Remembering that the angler himself may be visible to trout close to the riverbank it is advisable to make these initial casts from a few yards away from the water. As the line is cast further out the angler can advance forwards until he has covered systematically all the water within casting range of his stance.

Moving Regularly
It is then best to move upstream the requisite distance to cover a fresh patch of water. Thorough covering of the water in this way will ensure that any fish in the area is given an opportunity of rising to the fly, or flies. If there is no response, after several systematic presentations of the fly to likely feeding places for trout in this manner, the fly or flies may perhaps be changed as far as possible to correspond with any natural fly or flies on which the trout appear to be feeding.

Fishing from a bank on still water the angler can similarly cover the whole water within a 180 degree radius, before moving along to fresh water when it is felt the particular area has been flogged hard enough without result.

The Depth to Fish

The depth at which the artificial fly, nymph or bait is fished depends on a variety of factors. If the fish have ceased to rise, and are not taking any artificial flies offered near the surface, then the chances are that they are feeding near the bottom. A sinking line and the offer of some deeply sunk nymphs may make all the difference. When the sky is bright and the wind is light, with not a breath of air rippling the surface, the fish may well retreat to the depths and concentrate on feeding there. On the other hand, when there is a fine ripple on the surface and plenty of insect life about, the chances are that an artificial fly fished close to the surface may well prove successful.

The Water Itself

The state of the water, whether river or loch, is, of course, of the greatest importance. If there has been recent heavy rain and the water is brown and murky then fishing with an artificial fly may be next to hopeless. Then the only hope may be spinning with an artificial bait, or spoon, or else (in the final resort) worming. On the other hand, when the water is clear and there is little wind and the fish are rising, conditions may be ideal for using a dry fly, dropping it lightly so that it does not break the surface tension of the water, but sits up in an entirely natural fashion, landing close to the point where a feeding fish has been seen to rise. With a certain amount of wind, and a ripple on the water, a wet fly cast with the bob just touching the surface of the water at intervals may prove a certain means of catching trout.

Knowing the Water: The River

The advantages of knowing the water over which one is fishing cannot be over-stressed. If the fisher has walked or fished from a river bank at different times of the year and has seen the river when drought has reduced it to a mere trickle, or when floodwaters have been racing by in a surging flood, gouging out new sites for fish at each bend and overflowing on to nearby meadows, then he has a distinct advantage. He will know there are protected corners where the main current is diverted and a fish is likely to be able to lie in peace in a minor backwater. He will also know where rocks and fallen trees in the main stream, unseen when the river is at normal height, are also likely to provide similar shelter for trout and allow them to lie in wait for insects, larvae and other food drifting down in the current.

The Loch, Lake or Reservoir

As with a river or stream it is desirable, if possible, to know the underwater picture of a loch, lake or reservoir. The depths at which fish are likely to be feeding will vary according to outside factors such as weather, time of year, atmospheric conditions, feeding available and the size of the fish themselves. Any such water where there are islands or obvious shallows, or wherever a stream or inlet enters, or in the lee of any piers, promontories, or pensinsulas, is always likely to be a spot where fish will be found at certain times.

Still Water

The lake, the reservoir, the loch and the pond may all qualify as still water, as opposed to water with a current, but much depends on their size. A small lake, or reservoir, may be no larger than a lochan, or a pond, merely a matter of a few acres, only really fishable from the banks and barely worth the use of a boat. On the other hand a really large loch or lake, especially one with a river running into or out of it and surrounded by hills or open to the sea, may require a boat to be properly fished. Such large waters may also be subject to sudden considerable storms as the winds from surrounding hills funnel down on them, creating waves of a surprising size. Anyone who has had to bail out their boat in a hurry to avoid sinking in a storm in the middle of a large loch, as the waves lapped over the gunwale, would certainly query the title still water fishing in such circumstances. Yet here again a knowledge of the water and the depths below are of considerable importance to the fisherman. By studying the water at the various seasons of the year, and working out the depths of the various areas, it is possible to decide where the trout are most likely to feed at different times of day and during changes of temperature.

One Certainty
The only certain thing in trout fishing, however, is that the man who keeps trying in all conditions is likely to catch the most trout. On the other hand just blindly flogging the water is not likely to succeed. When nothing is happening it is as well to stop and ask oneself what one is doing wrong? Why are the trout not taking the fly? A change of fly size or fishing a little deeper or some similar simple alteration in fishing methods may make all the difference.

Spinning With Floating or Sinking Baits and Lures
There are various kinds of spinning bait or lure. There are those intended to move along more or less on, or just below, the surface without revolving, but zig-zagging erratically, and those which are meant to be fished at sometimes quite considerable depths, revolving as they do so, imitating the glitter of a swimming minnow. There is also the spoon type of bait, which may be a silver, golden or multi-coloured spoon shape with varying attachments. Perhaps the wooden, or hollow plastic lures designed to bob to the surface, but diving more deeply and zig-zagging more erratically the faster they are wound in, are among the more cunningly designed of floating baits or lures, as well as being the easiest to handle. They have the great advantage that when they snag an obstacle, such as stones in the bottom of a shallow patch of river bed, the chances are that when winding ceases they will bob to the surface. Sinking baits on the other hand, which are weighted both to carry them out further and to reach a suitable depth beneath the surface, tend to catch irretrievably in such obstacles.

The First Essential When Spinning

It does not matter what type of spinning bait is used, but a ball-bearing swivel should always be added to the end of the spinning line, with an anti-kink lead above it, or the line will inevitably soon twist and become useless. It is advisable also to add a leader of lower breaking-strain nylon from the swivel to the spinning bait. This ensures that if it sticks irretrievably on some obstacle on the bottom, as such baits often will, only the short leader is lost with the bait. Otherwise there is the danger that long lengths of nylon line from the reel may be lost. This can then very easily become disastrously wound round the legs of birds and mammals leading to a miserable death and is totally unforgiveable. Furthermore, fixed-spool reels are designed to work efficiently only with a full spool. Loss of any considerable length will necessitate renewing the entire reel. On all counts using a short leader of lower breaking-strain beyond the swivel is an essential and sensible safeguard.

The Basic Spinning Bait

As indicated there are certain baits, generally intended to imitate minnows, which have a small plastic or metal propeller in front causing them to revolve, or spin, through the water. They are known as Devons. These are now much less common than they were a decade or so back, but can still prove effective. The same may be said for the use of a dead minnow mounted on a spinner. The modern spoon type baits do not kink the line so readily but both do have the disadvantage that once caught on the bottom they are difficult to release effectively. This, however, is one of the perennial problems of spinning with almost any bait, especially in shallow water or where there are underwater obstructions. Both are also liable to catch salmon and other fish rather than trout.

The Use of Smell with a Bait

The idea of making an artificial bait more attractive to fish by the use of scents or essence is an old one. Aniseed, mashed minnow, or prawn and other similar mixtures are amongst those which have been recommended. Certain old types of Devons had a hollow body to be filled with such offerings. Occasionally modern variations are advertised as certain to attract fish. There may even be something in the idea.

Spinning Baits

The archetypal spinner is a freshly caught minnow mounted on a flanged spinner with a plastic or metal propellor in front of a central steel spike running through the body of the bait and wired hooks attached to it, but these are seldom seen nowadays, although still very effective in certain conditions. These and Devons are not likely to be of much interest to trout fishers, except possibly in search of Ferox when trolling, or spinning, at some depth. Basically they are intended for catching salmon, and anti-kink swivels will be necessary when using any of these to avoid the line twisting.

Wobblers

Baits such as the Toby and the Kynoch Killer are designed to wobble attractively under water. The Toby is made of metal and should be fished slowly or it may tend to spin, but otherwise its erratic movement in the water is most attractive to fish. The Kynoch Killer is of plastic and hollow. This has the advantage that it tends to float unless weighted and is thus useful in shallow water. Trout-sized baits of both kinds are available and can be useful. There are other similar baits on the market, but few as effective. Even with the smaller sizes, however, there is always the danger of catching salmon rather than trout.

The Spoon Bait

Just how the spoon bait evolved is hard to say, but the shape of a spoon without the handle does wobble most enticingly in the water when drawn through it on a line. It is from this basic design that all the modern vari-coloured spoon baits of silver, gold and facetted colourings, with their many varied bar attachments have developed. In certain circumstances the spoon bait can be deadly for trout. It is also likely to attract other fish such as perch and pike.

Mepps Spoons

There are a considerable variety of size and type of Mepps Spoons, which are now almost synonymous with the term 'spoon', and they are almost all effective killers. They have a flashing rotating fin which wobbles and also creates a vibration and attracts many varieties of fish, from salmon and trout to perch and pike. They are undoubtedly most effective. It is indeed one of the dangers of using them that you may find yourself with something very different to what you expected on the end of the line.

Spinning
Variable Speeds

The object of spinning is to imitate as far as possible the progress of a small minnow, or insect, working its way through the water. It is generally effective to move the bait, or lure, in a series of stops and starts, giving the general appearance of a small minnow moving erratically in short sharp rushes with zig-zag movements. This may also be reminiscent of a wounded fish, or damaged insect, making laborious progress through the water. The truly eager feeding trout may just catch a glimpse of it and dash forward without examining it too closely. It is a natural reaction for any fish to be attracted to the unnatural movements of a crippled prey and such bait or lure is likely to be preferred to one being simply wound in mechanically at a set speed. It is therefore a good plan to vary the speeds at which the bait or lure is wound, as well as halting occasionally to add to the reality of the effect. The depth at which the bait or lure is fished should also be varied with the same effect in mind. Sometimes it is better to fish deep and on other occasions nearer the surface. Much depends on the conditions prevalent on the day and of course the depth of the water itself.

Casting Up or Down Stream

In the normal course of events it is desirable to cast downstream and to cover the water between 9 and 12 o'clock across the stream, thus systematically covering the available water by degrees. The normal method would then be to move downstream to allow the next stretch of water to be covered systematically. Sometimes, however, it is necessary to cast upstream when, of course, the bait should at first be wound faster to compensate for the effect of the faster current until the 12 o'clock position is reached and the current begins to take effect against the bait allowing for a slower rate of retrieval to be effective.

Casting in Open Water

When spinning in open water from the bank of a loch or reservoir, or from a boat, there is, of course, a 180 degree area to cover and this should be done systematically from 9 o'clock to 3 o'clock or vice versa. If, however, spinning from a boat which is drifting downwind, or which is being rowed, this may become closer to a form of trolling and allowance must be made for the rate of movement to compensate for it.

The Depth for Spinning

The depth at which the spinning bait should be kept depends largely on the type of water being fished. Clearly in shallow water it is desirable to keep it clear of any possible obstructions where it may become caught. Where there are weeds or other obstructions it is clearly inadvisable to use a spinning bait. On the other hand it is quite feasible to spin quite close to the bottom of a river with a rocky bottom. In open waters it is largely a question of where it is felt the fish are likely to be most interested. This can often only be discovered by systematically varying the depth at which the bait is presented.

CHAPTER SIX

Trout Behaviour and Catching Them

Variations in Rises

It always pays to take time off to study the water before fishing. If the fish are seen to be rising all over the place that usually means the time is ripe to set up the rod and get to work. This is, however, not always the case. There are times when the trout may be seen rising freely but when they are not actively taking bait. The difference in the various forms or rise are clear enough after a little study.

The Feeding Fish

The trout which is coming to the surface and taking a fly makes a clear and distinctive circle of ripples behind. There is seldom much of a splash, but a widening circular ripple is left on the surface. The trout's nose may sometimes be seen to emerge, but in general all that is visible is the widening ripple left behind. Just occasionally an eager young fish, or a very greedy older one, may come clean out of the water and land with a resounding splash, but the same circle of ripples will be left.

The Boil

The boil is a distinctive rise by a large fish. It comes to the surface and swirls over its full length sometimes taking a fly in mid-air. The sight is always exciting and when it is taking a dry fly which has been presented to it successfully the sight is electrifying. This kind of rise is quite deliberate and there is no doubt that the trout intends to take firmly whatever it has in view.

The Splash

Frequently trout may appear to be rising, but if the rises are carefully watched it will be seen they are very splashy and on such occasions the trout are in fact merely playing at taking. They are in fact flapping at the surface with their tails. This form of rise can be very deceptive and usually indicates that the trout are not really hungry.

The Roll
It is also not uncommon to see the shoulders and back of a trout appearing above the surface, although the head itself does not appear. The trout may be feeding on nymphs or flies just below the surface of the water, and as it comes up to take them a large part of its body is exposed to view. This surface roll is indicative of where the trout may be feeding and a nymph or a dun fished just below the surface may prove successful.

Repeated Jumping
This sort of behaviour may arise with Sea trout fresh from the sea although it may also sometimes be seen with quite small trout leaping repeatedly from the water. In neither case does it necessarily mean very much. In the former case they may be trying to rid themselves of sea lice. In the latter they are probably not worth catching in any event.

Rising Trout
After a certain amount of experience it is possible to tell a considerable amount about what is happening on the water by the way the trout are seen to be rising. Although the novice might imagine that trout all rise in the same way this is far from true, as a little quiet observation during his early days of fishing will soon prove. In practice the way the fish are rising can often guide the angler correctly in his choice of fly, or bait.

The Tentative Circular Rise
In this instance the trout is just rising to the surface and delicately sucking in a small insect. It leaves a small circle of ripples and may seem to have been made by a small trout. In practice such small rises are often made by quite large trout of 2 or 3 pounds and it does not pay to judge them simply by the delicacy with which they have taken

an insect, very often in this case a dun. Rises of this kind are common close into the bank where a large trout has its station under some bushes or similar spot.

The Circular Rise and Bubble
A similar rise form which produces a more obviously pronounced circle is often seen to have a bubble in the centre. This indicates that the trout has sucked in a fly with a certain amount of air. When it turns head-onwards the air comes out of the gills and forms the bubble. This form of rise usually indicates the trout is taking a dun or spinner and has to reach out of the water to take it.

The Splashing Rise
When a trout takes a fly skittering across the surface of the water, or, for instance, a mayfly just leaving the water, it will often move in at speed, lifting its body half out of the water in its determination to gain its prize. Such a rise leaves a considerable commotion behind and when an artificial fly is taken in this way the reel starts to scream immediately.

The Clear Leap
Sea trout very often take in this manner, leaping clean out of the water to take the fly. This form of rise is also often seen where the trout are feeding on sedges. The leap is more often almost vertically out of the water, rather than horizontally as is the case with the Sea trout.

The Double Circle Rise
This rise is usually to be seen as two overlapping circles with their centres close together forming a kidney-shaped rise. It is generally agreed that this is caused by the trout rising in a rolling motion and taking a fly in the air before entering the water again. It is usually to be found when the large olives are present in the spring and autumn months.

The Explosive Rise
In this form of rise the trout may literally raise a white hump of water explosively in its determination to secure

a hatching nymph or other insect. This type of rise is easily recognised as it is quite different from any other. The angler at least knows that some form of hatching insect is being taken.

Other Ways of Identifying Feeding Trout

Underwater Feeding

The Torpedo Wave, the Bulge and Hump

Trout feeding underwater on nymphs or shrimps, especially over reed beds frequently make a fast torpedo-like wave on the surface as if they have been frightened, but once they have taken the nymph they will usually return to their previous station. When a trout sees a nymph passing just out of reach it may turn and dive after it, when its tail may cause a distinct bulge on the surface of the water. Sometimes when the trout is taking a nymph rising to the surface a distinct hump will be seen on the water, although the surface is not broken. This is caused by the trout executing a porpoise like head and tail roll in order to seize its prey.

Tailing

A trout feeding on nymphs and shrimps and similar food in the weeds, or silt, of the bottom will often stand on its head with its tail and fins maintaining its vertical head-downward position. This behaviour is difficult to see in any depth of water unless it is extremely clear and the observer is not visible. It can be observed easily enough in aquariums and is also readily seen in shallow water where the tail may be detected at intervals rising above the surface, hence the descriptive name.

Surface Feeding Trout

Head and Tail Feeders

When the nose of a feeding trout is seen to break the water for a moment, to be followed by the back and tail, it is feeding from the surface film and this may mean it has been attracted by any insect caught in that film, from duns and spinners, to shrimps and even sometimes nymphs in the process of changing.

Porpoise Roll Feeders

This form of rise is quite distinct from the head and tail rise and is much more exciting to watch, especially when the trout is in the act of taking a dry fly that has been cast over it. The trout arches its back as it comes up and the whole of the back is seen clearly before it submerges again, after probably taking a spent spinner.

Nymphing for Bottom Feeders

It is possible to cast a nymph, or indeed a wet fly, over a fish which is bottom feeding, tailing, or industriously cruising around some reeds in search of food, fairly repeatedly without frightening it, or in fact attracting its attention. Since the fish is busy searching for food, it is difficult to attract its attention and it is frequently a matter of luck that it sees the bait cast close to it and seizes it. The real difference between this form of fishing and dry fly fishing is that in the case of dry fly fishing the fish is feeding on the surface, and its whereabouts are plain. It is a comparatively simple matter to place the dry fly naturally in a position where the trout will see it and take it. When nymphing for a trout feeding in the weeds, or tailing, and industriously grubbing in the silt of the bottom, or in weeds, because its range of vision is much more restricted it is not easy to place the nymph in the right place to attract its attention.

Casting to a Rise Form in Fast Water

It is as well to appreciate that when casting to a rise form in reasonably fast-flowing water it is important to cast well forward since the trout is, of course, well upstream of where the rise form is seen to disappear. Although the rise form may be perfectly formed it can travel in that shape for several yards before disappearing. To cast too close to where it was thought to appear is almost certainly to cast behind the feeding trout and out of its field of vision.

Nymphing

In order to understand the principles of nymphing it is important to bear in mind the natural cycle and behaviour of the nymph. The artificial nymph may be fished either deep, or just below the surface with a floating line. Deep, in these circumstances is of course a relative term, since it may only be a foot or so beneath the surface, or it may be really well down towards the bottom. To be effective, however, the artificial nymph should be worked, either with the rod tip, or by jerking the line slightly with the left hand. In this way the artificial nymph beneath the surface appears to be imitating the actions of the natural insect struggling towards the surface.

Deep Nymphing

While deep nymphing in a river may mean only a matter of a foot or so beneath the surface, since the water is not much deeper, in a loch it may be a matter of fishing with a sinking line several feet down, but in each case the nymph is worked in the same way. Especially when fishing a loch nymphing is useful in flat calm conditions, or bright situations, when the fish appear to have gone off the feed altogether. The fact that they may sometimes take a nymph on these occasions quite steadily would seem to indicate that in such circumstances the trout have not actually stopped feeding, but have simply altered their feeding habits to suit the changed conditions. It is by working out what the trout are doing in different conditions and adapting his fishing methods accordingly that the imaginative angler catches fish where the fisher with a less flexible mind fails to do so. There is seldom any point in flogging the water when it is plain that the fish are not interested in what is being presented to them.

Nymphing Close to the Surface

When there is barely a ripple showing on the loch sufficient to fish successfully with wet flies a cast of artificial nymphs fished close to the surface can often be very successful. Fished just below the surface with a floating line, the technique is to imitate the natural actions of a natural nymph wearied by its struggles to reach the surface. The last foot or so, especially the final struggle to penetrate the surface film of the water, are when the nymph often appears at its most attractive to the feeding trout. After casting out, it is desirable to let the nymphs settle in the water with the floating line preventing them from sinking too deep. They should then be withdrawn very slowly and gently, just a few twitches at a time with the rod point or the hand on the line to simulate the struggles of the natural insect as it makes its way to the surface. The slightest sign of tension on the line is the signal to strike.

Nymphing Upstream in Fast Water
Although trout probably take just as many nymphs in fast water as they do in the slower and gentler currents of many southern rivers, upstream nymphing in such conditions is not really practicable. The speed of the current, the ruffled surface of the water, and the varied depths make it difficult to see what is happening and the speed of nymph returning towards the angler is much faster and more difficult to control properly. The probability, however, is that many trout take wet flies in such conditions under the impression that they are taking a nymph, for there is no doubt that some wingless wet flies look very like nymphs when sodden.

Wet Fly Techniques
The use of the wet fly on river or loch depends on circumstances. In a flat calm it is seldom, if ever, much use. The ideal conditions on a loch, or lake, are to have a slight ripple on the surface caused by a mild breeze. Too much wind makes for difficulties in casting and a flat calm is also undesirable since the fish will readily detect cast and angler. With a slight ripple to break the surface the trout are easily enough deceived by the wet fly.

Trout Behaviour
It is always worth studying both the behaviour of the trout and the variations in the water, or the different conditions and relating them together. Something can usually be learned in the process, but each day's fishing should produce some new, if seemingly insignificant, piece of knowledge. For instance, the behaviour of trout is likely to vary in different ways in different circumstances. In calm waters when stormy weather is approaching the

trout will usually go off the feed and retreat to the depths. In wilder, shallower running waters, in seemingly similar conditions, they may sometimes begin feeding eagerly. It may be that the water temperature has risen in the one case and not the other, or some such variable has not been taken into account, for, in general, trout behaviour tends to be explicable once all the factors are examined.

The Point of Maximum Concentration
When systematically covering the water on a river and mending the line at intervals to keep the fly or flies appearing as natural as possible, or when fishing still waters, the angler's attention should always be concentrated as far as possible on the fly or flies, if he can see them, or otherwise on the point where the line, or cast, enters the water so that he can detect the first sign of any movement. It is important to keep the line as nearly straight as possible between the slightly raised tip of the rod and the point where the line, or cast, is visible entering the water.

The Take
The magical moment when the fish is seen to rise and take the fly, or when the flies themselves suddenly disappear from view, or when the line is suddenly seen to disappear beneath the water before the reel begins to scream; those are the moments when that concentration can make the difference between catching or not catching the trout. Without that total concentration it is very easy to miss the moment when the fish comes to the flies. Sometimes there is a barely perceptible movement to indicate that the fish has taken a fly. Sometimes it is only a half seen movement, or gleam of the fish's belly in the water, which signals the moment.

Variations on the Take
The take may sometimes be signalled by a purposeful 'boil,' or splash, as the fish rises to the surface and takes the fly. Although sometimes a small trout can make a considerable splash, in general the larger the disturbance the larger the fish. Quite often with a dry fly, and sometimes even with a wet fly, the trout's head will be seen to come

out of the water and curl over to seize the fly with what sometimes seems a breathtaking slowness, and on such occasions it is possible to snatch the fly out of the trout's mouth before it has been swallowed by striking too soon. Although this type of take is common with salmon and quite frequent with a dry fly it is not so common with trout on the wet fly.

Striking
Striking is the term generally used for engaging the hook in the jaws of the trout once it is seen to take the fly. It is a somewhat misleading term for the novice since it is really a very minor, if definite, movement. Immediately the fish is seen to take the fly, the angler should respond by either simply raising or twitching the rod point and driving the hook firmly home. That is all that is meant by the term striking. If there is a good deal of line out it may be an improvement to strike simply by giving a short tug on the line held in the left hand, as well as raising the rod point. Lack of such response in time has meant many a good fish lost.

The Timing and Strength of the Strike
Apart from the one exception noted above it is almost impossible to strike too quickly when a trout has been seen to take the fly. Many trout are lost through failure to strike in time and allowing it to realise its mistake and spit out the hook before it has taken hold. Only once the fly has been firmly lodged by striking is it safe to start playing the fish. In his eagerness, however, sometimes the novice takes the word strike too literally and instead of just raising the rod tip literally flings the rod backwards with real force. This can result in an undersized trout hurtling out of the water and past the angler's ear to land some way behind him on the bank.

Breaking Strain
Alternatively, too heavy a strike may result in the hook tearing out of the trout's jaw, or the nylon of the cast breaking. It should be remembered that the breaking strain of the nylon on the cast next to the fly may often

be not more than 3 pounds and possibly a good deal less. Furthermore it may also have already been weakened by wear and tear. It is obvious that too much strain suddenly put on it by striking too hard with a large fish on the line may result in a broken cast and a lost fish, which may have been the only fish of the day and will certainly have seemed the largest. The only result in such cases will be to leave the fly and part of the cast in the trout's jaws. Fortunately this does not usually damage the fish unduly, since in general they will usually succeed in ridding themselves of this encumbrance in due course. It can, however, result in the trout catching the remains of the cast round some object such as a tree trunk and eventually being drowned. Moderation in striking, as in most matters concerned with fishing, is desirable.

Playing the Trout
Apart from the electric moment when the fish is actually being hooked there are few more exciting times than when the trout is actually being played. It is almost always desirable to put as much pressure on the fish as the rod and line will stand. Within reason the more pressure that can be put on the fish the better. In general many more fish are lost through letting them dictate terms than are lost through treating them firmly and keeping pressure on them continually. It is inadvisable to let the rod point drop too low, but keep it at about 2 o'clock so that the rod applies strain. If the trout is on a short line, however, do not raise the rod point too high since this will bring it nearer the surface and may cause it to fight harder. Keep the pressure on until you feel the fish begin to weaken, then bring him in and hold him so that the net can be slipped in quietly behind and under him before he realises what is happening. Do *not* bring him into towards the net so that he sees it and puts in a last struggle which if often enough to break the hold of the hook or even the cast itself.

The Leaping Trout
Should the fish rise to the surface and leap it is usually best to drop the rod point to one side and allow the line to

slacken momentarily before raising it again immediately. Otherwise it may happen that the trout falls across the taut cast and by its own weight drags the hook out of its jaw, or alternatively simply breaks the cast. This is the way in which many a trout, especially Sea trout, has been lost. If you have only a short line out and the fish leaps, for instance at the sight of the net, it is best to lift your rod hand and rod about a couple of feet straight up, then lower it as the fish returns to the water, thus retaining tension and not allowing the trout a chance to break the line.

'Giving it the Butt'
With the exception of a leaping trout pressure should generally be maintained at all times. It is by steadily applied pressure through correct use of the rod that the trout should be played. The expression 'giving it the butt' is meant to express this but it is not as many people seem to think by holding the rod upright that such pressure is exerted on the trout. With the butt of the rod in the stomach and the rod held at a comparatively low angle of around 2 o'clock the pressure on the fish is much greater than if the rod is held upright with the rod tip bending nearly double. The pressure is coming in the former case from the strongest part of the rod, i.e. the butt, and not as in the latter case from the much weaker part, i.e. the middle section. As the trout tires the line should be reeled in.

Use of Side Strain
When the trout has the opportunity of running under submerged logs or into weeds where the line may become entangled and the cast broken, it is essential to try to steer it away. The best method when it is desired to guide a fish in a required direction, e.g away from such dangers, is to hold the rod horizontally to one side so that the line is almost parallel to the water. Putting on steady pressure is then likely to bring the trout towards you. With the pressure kept evenly on the fish it is usually possible to walk steadily away from the direction of the immediate danger and in such circumstances the trout will usually follow.

Playing a Fish in the River

If the fish is hooked downstream, the angler should always try to get below it, or opposite it as soon as possible for it is then working against the current as well as the pressure of the rod. From upstream the angler is pulling against the current and against the trout's jaw, thus pulling the fly out of its mouth. When the trout runs up or downstream, follow as close as possible and keep the pressure on all the time.

Forcing a Fish to Move Up or Downstream

Try to position yourself opposite the trout and wait until he is temporarily quiet, then apply side strain and draw his head towards you, then walk slowly upstream or downstream always keeping ahead of the fish. This can be especially useful in the case of a very large trout, or to ease it away from dangerous places. Where there are weeds, or obstructions around, or a difficult stretch of water, this can be critical.

Pumping the Fish

A good way to put pressure on a trout and bring it into the net is by what is termed 'pumping'. This simply means keeping pressure on the trout and gradually raising the rod upright, then lowering the rod point quickly and reeling up the line as you do so, before then raising the rod point again and repeating the process. In this way even a strong fighting fish can be brought in to the net without too much trouble or strain on the rod.

The Effect of Applying Too Much Pressure

The method to avoid in such circumstances is the instinctive reaction to apply as much pressure as possible with the rod held upright. Although this may be effective if rod and cast are sufficiently strong it will probably cause the trout to feel it is being dragged towards the surface and will merely result in it fighting harder and boring away downwards in the opposite direction. It is equally likely to result in the hook losing its hold or the cast breaking under the strain.

Dealing with a Fish in a Weed Bed

If a fish has managed to take cover in a weed bed it is not usually a good plan to try to put pressure on him as this is likely to make him bury himself more deeply in the weeds. There are two ways of dealing with the situation: either let him have plenty of line so that he is not fussed and may try to free himself, or else get well downstream and try handlining, i.e. putting the rod down or pointing the rod at the fish and hauling the line in by hand at near water level, if the cast is strong enough to take the strain. This may work as the fish does not feel the strong pressure in the same way—but it can also end in a broken cast and a lost fish.

The Foulhooked Fish

A fish that is foulhooked in the tail, fins, or back is likely to feel very heavy and will usually take a lot longer than normal to tire. If foulhooked in the side or elsewhere he may be very excitable. It is usually simply a question of being patient and tiring him out before netting.

Bringing the Trout to the Net

The aim should be to play the fish and tire him so that gradually more and more line can be retrieved. After the first fierce rushes the struggles are likely to grow less determined until the angler knows that he has control. Once this stage has been reached and the line shortened sufficiently a steady applied pressure should be sufficient to bring the trout within reach of the net.

Netting

It is important not to become too confident at this stage. It has often enough been the case that as the angler brought the fish up to the net the sight of it has caused the fish to make a last desperate struggle, and the fast, or the hold of the hook in the jaw, weakened by the fight, has parted to allow the trout to escape. There are few sights more heartbreaking than seeing the only, and of course the largest, fish of the day swimming off while almost within reach of the net. On the river it is desirable therefore to wait until the fish is well under control before slipping the net gently into the water, and then allowing the trout to slide slowly backwards towards the sunken net before sweeping it underneath and scooping the net and trout together onto the bank. In still waters it is desirable to sink the net well beforehand and, if possible, play the fish until the head can be raised slightly from the water as it is drawn over the mesh before scooping it upwards.

Mistakes in Netting
To bring the net towards the trout within its field of vision is asking for a final desperate struggle. With a fish larger than the diameter of the net it is always desirable to slide him in tail first. In any event the net should always be sunk well into the water before bringing the trout near it. Once the fish is fairly and squarely into the net it should be swung in one movement into the boat or on to the bank. Hesitation at this moment can often be fatal, for many trout have been lost at the last moment when the pressure of the line has been eased and the hook gave way before the net was properly in position. Sadly such lack of co-ordination and control is more likely to happen after a lengthy struggle with a large trout, when the concentration is at last weakened with the imminent approach of victory, than with a small trout when there has been little or no struggle involved.

Dealing with the Catch
Despatching
Once the trout is ashore, or in the boat, it is usually desirable to kill it promptly, for, quite aside from the question of needless cruelty, a large fish floundering around once detached from the hook has been known to leap overboard again, or wriggle off the bank and back into the water. To kill any trout the best method is a sharp blow with a heavy blunt instrument (e.g. a priest) at the back of the head behind the gills.

Returning to the Water
If the trout is not required for eating or to fill a bag limit and it is felt that it has put up a good fight and deserves returning to its native element; or alternatively, if it is

under-sized and it is felt it should be put back to learn more sense and grow up then it is advisable to keep the handling to a minimum. It is best, if possible, to keep the trout in the net in the water and try to shake the hook free. If, however, the hook is deeply imbedded it may be necessary to twist it free and in such cases the less the trout is handled the better for it is handling outside the water and removal of the essential oils and scales which affect its chances of survival adversely and cause disease, so that not only may it die a few days later, but it may infect others. It is for this reason that commercial trout fisheries have differing rules. Some sensibly insist on killing each trout caught up to the bag limit. Others require the use of barbless hooks after catching the bag limit. Yet others insist on using barbless hooks only.

Transporting Trout
Once the trout is caught, safely netted and killed, it is desirable to keep it in the best condition. A plastic bag with some water inside it is a suitable means of keeping it in good condition and this is easily carried in a boat. When fishing on river bank or loch or lakeside, this can sometimes be deposited safely at some well-marked spot and the catch placed in it preparatory to picking it up when returning home. This is a better and more satisfactory method than carrying them in the fishing bag itself which otherwise soon becomes extremely smelly.

CHAPTER SEVEN

Different Waters Different Approaches

Large Lochs, Lakes and Reservoirs
The complete novice faced with a seemingly vast expanse of water is understandably very often completely at a loss to know where to start. In such circumstances, however, there are certain rules which are almost always applicable. The first of these is that trout will always go wherever the best feeding is available. There may be some trout found elsewhere, but they will be scarce and probably, by corollary, thin.

The Prevailing Wind
In any large expanse of water the prevailing wind inevitably blows a good deal of insect and other food towards one shore or the other. It is here that the bulk of the trout will go for their food and it is here that the angler should try his luck for a start. If fishing from the bank the angler should not be surprised if the fish are feeding well within casting range, quite close to the edge. This form of fishing may mean casting into the wind, but it is usually quite convenient to cast at an angle to the bank, covering the available water steadily while slowly moving forward.

Wading
If it is possible to wade close in shore and the angler decides to do so this may be preferable to standing on the bank silhouetted against the water and possibly alarming the fish. When wading it is desirable to move slowly, to avoid splashing and once again alarming the fish. If the shore shelves abruptly, of course, wading may be out of the question.

Fishing from a Boat
When fishing from a boat the ideal is to drift steadily before the wind on a line close enough to the shore to cover

the water adequately. In general the trout will probably be feeding quite close inshore, but it is usually a good plan to cover the area where the water starts to deepen. Between there and the shoreline itself the trout are likely to be feeding when the conditions are most suitable for them, i.e. when the atmospheric and water conditions are right and when the insect life or other feed is present.

Likely Feeding Places
Wherever trees or bushes, particularly any bearing fruit or berries, overhang the water there are likely to be trout feeding on insects that have been attracted to them or fruit that has fallen from them. Similarly, wherever a feeder stream or minor tributary enters the water there are likely to be trout feeding on insects, larvae or other food that has been washed down. Then again any small bays, or pools, formed by indentations in the bank, are also likely to provide richer feeding and will be worth fishing carefully. Finally, any promontory, even a jetty, sticking out into the water, is likely to have some trout using it for shelter and as their particular territory.

Likely Feeding Times
From April and May on to September and October, depending on the location, trout may generally be seen to start rising freely and feeding at fairly regular times in the morning and in the evening when there is a natural hatch of flies. These regular feeding patterns may be affected by changes in the weather pattern, for instance storms affecting atmospheric conditions, but even so some fish are likely to be ready to feed at these times. A somewhat similar effect may be noticed in regularly stocked commercial waters during the winter months when the bulk of the fish tend to remain in the depths and have less energy and urge to take a fly or lure as in the warmer part of the year. Then the recently introduced stock fish tend to remain in shoals near the surface and are more inclined to feed at the times they were normally fed in the fishery, usually around 8 or 9 in the morning and 3 or 4 in the afternoon. Although their behaviour has been imposed

artificially they are really following a natural pattern and lifestyle prior to adapting to conditions in the wild.

Reading the Water

The ideal when fishing from a boat is to have a map of the water showing the varying depths and shallows, otherwise a knowledge of the underwater terrain can only be roughly guessed. A careful eye on the shoreline, however, should indicate where the shore shelves steeply and where the ground is likely to extend further under water providing shallows. Shallower water will usually be clearly advertised by a lighter colouring and other indications, such as reeds or other growth, may be apparent. Any island will probably have shallower water around it, and so generally will promontories or peninsulas of land jutting into the main water. In clear conditions, of course, it may simply be a matter of watching the bottom through the water.

Drifting

The general principle observed when fishing from a boat in a loch or lake is to allow the boat to drift slowly downwind in the general line it is desired to fish. Laying the boat sideways on the wind is a simple enough matter with the oars left securely in the rowlocks. After a little practice it becomes a simple enough matter to control the line of the drift with one oar while casting at the same time with the other hand. The ideal conditions for a wet fly, whether fishing from the bank or from a boat are to have slight ripple on the water caused by a mild breeze. In conditions such as these it is a comparatively simple matter to drift down the chosen area where the shallows merge gradually with the deeper water, usually clearly visible as a darker line beneath the water. When fishing with two rods the usual method is for one to fish the area over the deeper water and the other to fish up to the shoreline. The bob fly should be allowed just to dangle in the ripple and the line should be drawn back steadily to match and slightly exceed the speed at which the boat is drifting.

Playing a Fish from a Boat

When there are two rods in a boat and a fish is caught the other rod should promptly reel in and help by taking the oars and trying to keep the boat at right angles to the fish. It is desirable to try to keep the fish always facing the same way he was caught to avoid undue wear on the hold of the hook, so the boat should when possible be turned accordingly. If it is caught in shallow water apply side strain and try to lead it into deeper water to play it. In open water where there are no obvious dangers such as weeds, let the trout run by all means, but keep a steady pressure. Should it run towards the boat do not allow the line to go slack, but take it in quickly, maintain the pressure and be ready for another run. When the trout approaches the boat the oarsman should try to row further away and the angler should try to keep him away by applying side strain. If the fish nevertheless tries to go underneath it is sometimes worth stamping on the bottom of the boat to prevent it. If the trout succeeds in getting underneath the boat do not hesitate but thrust the rod point and line deep under the bow or stern, whichever is nearest, and bring the line clear on the other side. It is never desirable to try to play the trout right under the point of the rod close to the boat as this is inviting trouble.

Landing a Fish from the Shore

When fishing from a boat close to the bank and even when wading it is often worth going ashore and landing the fish from there once it has been played to the point of exhaustion. It is usually safer and more effective than trying to net it in the water, especially if it is a big trout.

Boat Fishing with a Drogue

In order to slow the rate of drift when there is a stiff breeze it is a good plan to have a drogue handy. Some fisheries provide well-made canvas or nylon cloth drogues with the boats. A makeshift drogue is easily constructed by lashing two pieces of wood in the form of a cross and slipping the ends through an old fertiliser bag with a hole cut out of its bottom. With a rope attached to the centre of the cross this will act as a sea anchor and slow the rate of drift considerably. Even a spare pair of oars lashed together may act as a makeshift drogue or sea anchor at a pinch. The more line attached to the drogue the deeper it will sink and the slower the rate of drift, but do not forget that the water may not be of the same depth and it is not desirable for the drogue to tangle on the bottom.

Drifting with One Angler
It may take a little practice but the singlehanded angler will find that it is quite feasible to drift sideways on to the wind with both oars firmly in the rowlocks. It only requires an occasional tug on one or other oar to keep the boat drifting in the required direction once the technique has been mastered. The angler can in fact control the boat one-handed while still casting with his free hand, or even when playing a fish, but practice is required for those who are not naturally boat-minded.

Drifting with Two Rods Bows First
Drifting with two rods, with or without a boatman, requires a certain co-ordination between the anglers. If drifting bows first then the technique is for each angler to take a separate side of the boat. If each casts over the shoulder furthest away from his fellow angler there should be little chance of them catching each other and getting their lines entangled. When one or other is into a fish, however, it may be advisable, although by no means always necessary, for the other to stop fishing. If they have no boatman it may be agreed as a matter of courtesy for the angler not actively playing a fish to act as boatman and net the catch, but again this is a matter for mutual agreement.

Drifting with Two Rods Broadside On
In this case much depends on the length of the boat. In the usual 12 foot clinker-built loch boat there is little danger of the anglers catching each other if, once again, each casts on the side furthest away from his fellow angler. Where they feel it may be advisable, however, they may warn

each other with a cry of 'casting now' whenever about to cast, in order to avoid any entanglements.

Good Boating Manners in the Boat
There are certain points which it is always worth remembering when fishing from a boat. Sticking to those noted above will ensure that there should be no entanglements when fishing with a partner in a boat. Above all avoid the heinous crime of casting across the line of the other's cast even if you see a fish rising temptingly which he appears to have overlooked. Standing up in a boat at any time is not just bad manners but sheer stupidity, and is asking to capsize the boat or fall overboard. Do not knock out a pipe on the side of the boat or drop heavy objects noisily inside it, and never have a radio playing loud music in the boat, or on the bank. This is quite enough to frighten all the fish for a good distance around.

Good Boating Manners when Drifting the Boat
Do not cut in on someone else's drift, but slip in behind them at a reasonable distance if that is the drift you want to take. Do not approach the shore where there are bank anglers casting. Always keep out at least twice their casting range from the bank or you will be interfering with their sport. Similarly do not take the boat inshore where anglers are fishing unless they happen to be fishing from your mooring jetty. If you are fishing from an anchored position and a boat is following a drift that will come close to you it is probably courtesy for the anchored boat to move and allow the drifting boat to move through.

Fishing from Anchor
There are occasions when it is simply best to anchor the boat in an obviously sound chosen spot and fish from it rather than take what looks like being a totally unproductive drift. For instance a bay may be full of weed and unfishable but the outside edge may be extremely productive. Similarly the wind may be blowing directly towards a high dam wall against which the trout are busily feeding, but where it is impossible to drift. It may also sometimes be worth dropping the anchor to slow the rate

of drift and halt for a moment or two in a productive area. Partially dropping the anchor so that it acts as an aid to the drogue is also sometimes worthwhile when the drogue itself is not entirely successful.

Striking

In the boat the angler's eye should always be on the point where the line enters the water and at the slightest hesitation or check he should strike immediately by raising the rod point, for loch or lake trout, especially when there is only a very little ripple, are often very shy takers, barely doing more than mouthing the fly before ejecting it. It is indeed often the case that they may be seen following the fly and inspecting it carefully before taking it, but in such circumstances they will usually take it greedily enough when they do decide to do so.

Regular Casting from a Boat

Due heed should be taken of the speed of drift and the casting matched to it so that the fly is drifting on or in the water in as natural a manner as possible. Depending on the rate of drift this may mean casting and retrieving the line surprisingly fast at times. It is also important to try to cover the water evenly in front of the boat so that as much water as possible is fished. Thus it may be advisable to cast forward with the first cast and then cast at an angle sideways with the next cast thus covering two different areas during the period that the boat takes to drift over them. Clearly the more area that can be covered the more the chances of catching a hungry fish.

Boating Hazards

In any large lochs or stretches of water surrounded by mountainous country it is always advisable to have a care. Storms can blow up surprisingly quickly and getting caught in deep water with a full gale blowing and waves breaking over the side of the boat is not a pleasant experience. Nor is it desirable to be caught in such circumstances in a thunderstorm with lightning liable to strike the metal rings of the rod, especially as carbon fibre, or any wet rod, is a very good electrical conductor. In such circumstances discretion is the better part of valour, and it is wiser to head for the shore or home, whichever is the nearest. In any event fishing in such circumstances is generally a waste of time.

Shallow Water

Where there is a large bay, or for some other reason a large area of shallow water, as is found occasionally in both lochs and reservoirs, it may be necessary to wade a considerable distance before reaching the area where the water begins to darken and deepen, which is often favoured by feeding trout. The temptation in such circumstances is to feel that the further one can cast the more likely the chances of success, and admittedly some large trout may be taken in this way in the deeper waters, but it is equally true that more trout will probably be found in the areas closer to the bank. There is an incurable angler's malaise which ensures that the further out of range a stretch of water may be, the more certain it seems that there the large fish are waiting to be caught.

Fishing in a Dead Calm

Fishing with a wet fly on a loch, lake or reservoir when there is absolutely no wind at all and the water is gleaming like a burnished mirror is to all intents and purposes a waste of time. It is then the dry fly, the nymph and similar lures come into their own. When the fish start feeding it is also an object lesson to learn how many trout there are in waters that may previously have seemed completely devoid of fish. Accurate casting from boat or bank to individual feeding fish is then the most effective method of catching trout. It is important, however to find out first what they are feeding on and provide as close an imitation of the natural fly as possible.

Dapping

In sunny conditions usually in May, June, or even later in the season, with a goodish wind raising a sizeable wave, when the wet fly is not proving successful, another method somewhat akin to dry fly fishing known as dapping can sometimes prove an exciting method of catching trout.

This can be practiced from a boat, or when wading, or even in some circumstances from the bank or from a bridge. Although a longish rod is an advantage, and dapping rods of 14 feet or so used to be common enough and may still be found in places, an ordinary rod with a light line will probably suffice. A special floss line is used to attach a large dapping fly to the line. A mayfly is often used but a large sedge, or a Great Gnat (i.e. a Daddy-Longlegs) will generally work well. The object is to allow the wind to take the fly well out and allow it to dance on top of the waves in the manner of a genuine insect just touching the surface of the waves occasionally. The principle is that the floss catches the wind and causes the fly to dance on the water in a tantalising manner. In this way some surprisingly large trout may be caught in what would otherwise seem extremely unfavourable conditions. It is, of course, possible to use this method of fishing successfully in smaller lochs or lakes and even on larger rivers as well, given suitable conditions. There may even be occasions when it may be worth trying this or a similar method in suitable pools, in smaller burns or streams, from a riverbank or from a bridge. It never pays to leave any method of fishing untried when others are not working.

The Larger Rivers
Underwater Contours and Snags

As with the larger lochs and reservoirs it is desirable to know the underwater contours of any large river. Since, of course, this is liable to alter each season with the effects of floodwaters during the winter and spring months, a good deal has to be guesswork, although the angler who fishes any stretch of river regularly will learn valuable lessons during periods of drought and low water. The presence of invisible underwater snags and obstacles, which can otherwise only be learned the hard way by losing fish or cast, will then be revealed. To the angler who is fishing the water for the first time such hazards may only be guessed at by swirling currents on the surface of the water, or by a branch or rock protruding apparently innocently in the water.

Overlong Casting

As with any water the angler will do well to avoid the temptation arising from the niggling certainty that the largest fish are lying in water which is just beyond casting range. The pools under the opposite bank in clear view always seem certain to contain the best trout in the river and it is easy to ignore the fact that seen from the opposite bank the pools on this side look equally enticing. Careful study of the water and steady covering of the likely spots close at hand are always liable to be far more productive than frenzied overlong casting in an attempt to cover tempting areas beyond sensible reach. The end result of such efforts is usually to hook a tree or bush, either on the back cast, or on the far bank, and lose the fly or cast.

Systematic Casting

When fishing, whether wet or dry fly, from the bank or wading it is important to cast systematically, unless casting to an individual fish. A good deal must depend on the amount of current in the water. The ideal is to cover the area from where the stance has been taken up from 10 or 11 o'clock across the water to 3 o'clock downstream by degrees, starting with the area close at hand and lengthening the line by degrees until the whole area within casting distance has been covered, and the cast with fly or flies has been allowed to drift as naturally as possible over the whole available area. When approaching the water therefore it is desirable, if possible, to stand back from the bank so that neither the angler, nor the movement of the rod, is visible to a fish lying close in to the side. It is surprising how often a large trout is to be found lying close in or even under the bank and an incautious approach can easily alarm it. Once this area has been covered the next stretch a few yards further out should be covered and so on until the angler has covered the river as far as his casting abilities will allow. If this finally permits the angler to cast comfortably, so that the fly or flies land below the opposite bank well and good, but if he cannot reach this without overlong casting, or wading out of his depth, then this area should be ignored.

Upstream Fishing

Upstream wet fly fishing or nymphing can often prove surprisingly effective, but once again careful and systematic coverage of the water is essential. Here the angler must retrieve his line steadily at the same rate as the current and be careful to keep the cast as far as possible in a straight line so that the fly or nymph appears as natural as possible to the trout. This is very similar to fishing wet fly from a boat and the cast must be watched carefully for the first sign of any tension, when the rod tip should be promptly raised and the strike should prove effective.

Likely Lies

It is well worth studying the sort of places trout like to lie in wait for their food. Any small obstruction, a rock, patch of weeds, or a curve in the riverbank where an eddy occurs and a trout may find some protection from the current is the sort of place where trout are most likely to be found. They will in general lie facing the current waiting for insects, small crustacea or similar food to float down over them. Their field of vision is limited to the water and surface area almost immediately above them in a semi-circular area. The angler's aim therefore should always be to float his fly, or lure, down over these areas in as nearly a natural manner as possible. Whether he is casting upstream, or across the water and allowing the fly to drift down, it must be obvious that although different methods may be required to present the fly, the end result should be that it drifts over the trout looking as natural as possible.

The Dry Fly

There are times even on a large river when the dry fly is the only answer, but on rivers of any size there is always the problem of the line bellying, resulting in constant line mending to avoid drag. Even so there are bound to be places where the current is slow and the dry fly can come into its own. Where the trout can be seen to rise quite clearly, and are leaving distinct marked circles behind them, the situation is ideal for the dry fly. Even where the rise is lost almost immediately the dry fly can provide very good sport, but remember to allow for the current when casting where the rise was seen.

The Dry Fly and The Rising Trout
Unless deliberately casting over feeding trout the normal approach to fishing with the dry fly is little different from that used when fishing with a wet fly. The principle should be to cover the water systematically starting with the area closest at hand and ending up by casting as far as conveniently possible compatible with allowing the fly to float naturally with the current, until such a stage as it begins to drag unnaturally in the water. There is this difference that should a fish be seen to rise at any stage

STALKING A RISING TROUT WITH DRY FLY

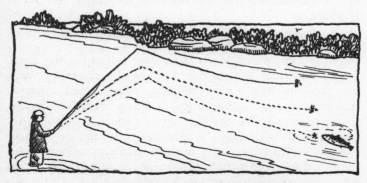

WET FLY FISHING (DOWNSTREAM)

110

in the proceedings it is well worth making an immediate cast and attempting to cover the rise in the hope that the fish will be in the mood for taking it. While some might advocate taking similar action with wet flies it is probably only worth doing so when a fish is seen to be rising repeatedly.

Fishing from a Boat

Fishing a river from a boat is a very different proposition from fishing a loch, or lake. To begin with, a boat on a river is necessarily always restricted to a given stretch, or beat. There is seldom any question of the angler acting as his own gillie or boatman and rowing himself as well as fishing. The object of the boat is to enable the angler to reach water that it would be next to impossible to cover by wading, even with chest waders. The gillie, who naturally knows his water intimately, will probably cover the water rather like a pointer covering its ground in search of game, zig-zagging backwards and forwards, or else taking a stretch on each side at a time, before rowing back upstream in the weaker current to start afresh. In some rivers a rope, chain, or anchor may be used to let the boat down slowly and prevent the current taking complete control. In other rivers the gillie rowing against the current may be enough to allow the boat to drift gently downstream covering the desired water. Such boats are usually reserved for salmon fishing only, but it may be that in exceptional cases they could be used for trout fishing.

Variations

When fishing wet fly downstream it often pays to work the fly or flies, i.e. jerk them through the water by moving the rod tip sharply, or, when in a patch of rougher water, pulling on the line with the spare hand, thus attracting the attention of a trout and tempting it to dash at the fly. Whenever the sun is shining brightly advantage should also always be taken of any patches of shade on the water cast by trees or bushes on the bank. By letting the flies deliberately drift from light to shade an otherwise uninterested trout may sometimes be attracted to the cast. When nothing else seems effective and conditions are for instance bright, sunny and unhopeful, it is sometimes worth investigating likely looking patches and using unorthodox methods. For instance almost every river contains pools where one or other bank has been undercut and there may be undergrowth or vegetation growing above it. It is often worth fishing such places, where large trout are likely to be lying, with some unusual lure such as an imitation of a land-borne insect like a spider or caterpillar. Some such lure, dropped quite splashily on the surface, may prove effective and some memorable trout have been caught by such methods. It may even be worth dapping if the conditions seem suitable for it.

The Smaller River

Quite when a river becomes classified as small is largely in the eye of the beholder and what he is accustomed to fishing. Clearly, however, a river where one might require a boat to fish the beats, or where chest waders are required for fishing in order to reach the far bank may reasonably be termed large. When it is possible to cast from one side to the other, with only minimal wading, it is certainly a great deal smaller and may be regarded as in a smaller, if no less interesting, category. It is even the case that some smaller rivers have the well deserved reputation of providing better and more interesting fishing, as well as sometimes larger fish, than much larger rivers. It is both invidious and almost impossible to compare, for instance, a highland spate river such as the Findhorn and a small chalk stream in Dorset such as the Piddle, yet each can produce superb trout fishing of quite different kinds. Each can be fished from bank to bank with ease. Yet to try to compare the sport that each provides let alone to compare them with larger rivers is irrational and absurd, like comparing an elephant with a lion: while each is a mammal with four legs, they have practically nothing else in common. So it is with many rivers large and small.

Chalk Stream Fishing

Chalk streams may vary enormously in size, just as any other waters, but are mainly found in the south with a scattering as far north as Yorkshire. The fish in such streams are likely to be well fed and fairly evenly distributed through-out the water. The water is generally clear and the current is not immediately obvious, although sometimes quite considerable. The fish may be found lying under cover of reed beds, around inlet streams, or close to bridges, weirs and similar obstructions. The fishing is generally restricted to dry fly or to upstream nymphing. With any rise visible it is generally a question of stalking the feeding fish and casting the fly so that it floats over him in as natural a manner as possible. Then with fortune favouring the angler there is the heart-stopping moment when the trout is seen to take the fly and the fight is on. While this can prove amongst the most expensive of trout fishing in the United Kingdom there are many who will claim that it provides full value for money. It can cost anything up to £50 or more a day in some areas, but for those who can afford it, it is probably worth the money and there are generally fishing clubs through whose membership such fishing may be obtained very much more cheaply.

Well Stocked Waters
While it is easy to see that put-and-take fishing carried to extremes can be anathema to any sportsman worthy of the name it is understandable enough that anyone offering fishing for sale has to keep his waters stocked with sufficient fish to keep up with the demand. Even with a firmly enforced bag limit any loch, or lake, which has a regular number of anglers removing fish from the water each day must replenish its stocks at fairly frequent intervals. The effect, of course, is that most of the fish introduced as replenishments into these waters are straight from artificial fish ponds where they have been bred, and are totally inexperienced. There is a very fine line that has to be drawn at this point between keeping the waters reasonably well stocked and introducing too many. If the balance is not correctly maintained and the waters are over-stocked it is clear that once again the angler may be catching fish with little or no conception of life in the wild. It is true that as an introduction to fishing this may seem to be the perfect way for a beginner to start. Whether in some instances it may not be making it too

easy, inculcating a false sense of values and introducing a false concept of sportsmanship is another matter. It is up to every individual to decide such matters for himself. Conscience is entirely a matter for each individual.

Stocking the Water
The balance of nature in most waters has been so disturbed by over-fishing that careful re-stocking at intervals is one of the most important features of any fishing. It is easy, as indicated, to overdo it and this is just as disastrous as not stocking sufficiently. There are, it has to be admitted, few things more dispiriting than fishing steadily in promising-looking trout water where there are only a few wary old specimens, all cannibals with lean bodies and large heads. To start in such circumstances is disheartening for any beginner and something between the two extremes is the ideal answer.

Fishing the Estuary
There is one form of fishing that surprisingly few regular trout fishers have experienced. This is fishing the estuary waters of a river or loch where the salt and fresh waters mix. In practice there will be a noticeable rise and fall with the tide of many rivers and sea lochs even 2 or 3 miles or more from the sea and the water will have a slightly briny flavour if tasted. In such waters both Brown trout and Sea trout may be encountered. A strange variety of sea and freshwater fish may also be caught at times, rising unexpectedly to the fly. Grayling, perch, flounders, even mackerel close in to the shore and other unexpected catches may be made at times.

The Sea Trout
Fishing for Sea trout is perhaps the most satisfying form of trout fishing, but sadly, as with salmon, the stocks of Sea trout seem to be steadily diminishing in many areas where at one time they were regularly to be found at certain seasons of the year. There are various reasons suggested for this, such as too much and too frequent netting at river mouths, drift netting too close inshore, disease caused by ill-managed fish farming and greedy over-fishing by rod

fishermen both in the rivers and estuaries. Both drift netting at sea, a deadly form of fishing which undoubtedly has affected stocks of salmon and Sea trout, and disease, whether caused by inefficient fish farming or from other causes, have undoubtedly taken their toll, and now it is up to the sporting angler to play his part in conserving stocks by avoiding the less sporting methods of catching Sea trout.

Knowledge of the Water
The greatest advantage any angler can have in catching trout, but more especially Sea trout, is a sound knowledge of the river or loch. Knowing the various pools and particularly the usual depth of the water in them, also when it is best fished after there has been a spate, gives such an angler a considerable edge on anyone who is only an infrequent visitor and who has as a result to rely on local advice, some of which may not always be disinterested. In such circumstances a gillie who can be relied on and who knows his water thoroughly is not only worth his pay, but should earn every penny of it.

Some General Points
The point to remember is that Sea trout are travelling fish, unlikely to be found for long in the same place, but steadily moving upstream. A river of any length over, say, 10 miles will always hold a certain number of Sea trout, but they will be constantly on the move upstream, as the height of the water allows them to do so. These shoal Sea trout are usually to be found in daylight sheltering under the bank, the larger ones in the deeper pools. During the day they will usually be found near the head of the pools and at night they tend to slide back to the tail of the pools. Of course circumstances may alter cases, but this will usually turn out a good rule of thumb to work on.

The Cautious Approach
While caution is always advisable when fishing for trout this is even more essential when it comes to fishing for Sea trout. It is necessary to approach the edge of the bank extremely cautiously and cast with great care. Noise and

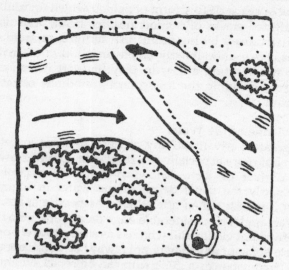

FISHING THE DRY FLY (UPSTREAM)

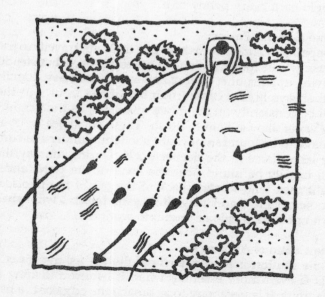

FISHING THE WET FLY (DOWNSTREAM)

disturbance of any sort is fatal. There is a river I know quite well which is readily fishable from either bank, although occasionally one or other may be overgrown, but seldom both. It has regular Sea trout runs but they appear to be caught very seldom for the simple reason that the majority of anglers who fish the river tend to wade up the middle in thigh waders. The result is that all the Sea trout are very thoroughly alarmed and few are caught, at least by anglers such as these.

Fly Sizes
The flies used to catch Sea trout will generally be several sizes larger than those used for ordinary Brown trout and the flies chosen should be the customary Sea trout patterns such as the Alexandra, Peter Ross, Mallard and Red, and Teal and Red or similar recognised Sea trout favourites. A selection of such flies set on heavier cast with a breaking strain of around 6 or 8 pounds is probably suitable for most conditions. There are inevitably, however, local favourites in every area which will be strongly recommended and which are likely to be worth trying. It is an interesting point that there is a decided similarity at times, not only between the lures used for Sea trout and for large Rainbows, but also in the method of fishing with them. Rainbow can in fact frequently be caught with large Sea trout lures when they are otherwise hard to move from the deeper water which they frequently prefer.

Night Fishing
One of the really fascinating aspects of Sea trout fishing is fishing for them in the darkness, or semi-darkness of midsummer months. They tend to be eager night feeders and virtually the only way to catch them at times is to fish late at night and through towards dawn. This type of fishing has its own attraction. It is important to know one's ground and prospect it well in daylight. It is also essential to stick to a cast of one or at the most two flies. The sound of the Sea trout rising, usually in the slower water can be tantalising, but even at night care is required to keep out of sight and avoid presenting a silhouette against the sky if possible. It is advisable to keep a short line and cover

the water carefully, especially the shallows, where the Sea trout are often to be found. To hear the sound of the rise and suddenly feel the rod and line under intense pressure is a moment of ever recurring excitement. Playing the fish with only the silvery splashes and the bending of the rod to indicate where it is to be found, results inevitably in many heart-stopping moments. Sudden silvery splashes with a quivering bar of silver skittering on the surface amongst them are often all one has to see when a Sea trout is leaping repeatedly over the surface of the water. It can be largely a matter of guesswork as to exactly what is happening at times, and when the fish is finally brought safely into the net it is a moment of intense satisfaction even for the most experienced of anglers. It is well worth losing a little sleep to secure a good bag of Sea trout in the hours of darkness and most such occasions remain in the memory long after more ordinary days' fishing are forgotten.

In Tidal Waters

The effect of the tide is all important in tidal waters. Around an hour either side of high water the Sea trout are likely to start moving and taking freely. When this combines, in northern waters, with the hours of dusk or dawn in the midsummer months, then conditions are usually just about perfect and good sport can be confidently expected. The combination of rising tide and darkness make for perfect conditions. The best lures are probably tube flies and what are termed terrors, i.e. double flies mounted on a short thick piece of nylon, with the trailing wing of the front fly lying back an inch or so to cover the second fly as well. Both these flies tend to shimmer and wiggle in the water and at times seem almost irresistible when fishing estuary waters.

After The Spate

When there has been a long dry spell during which Sea trout and salmon have been unable to work their way up the river to their spawning beds, a prolonged spate will bring them up river in large numbers. While the water is still brown and opaque, so that no fly stands a chance of being seen, the Sea trout can only be caught with a worm. The method used is almost exactly the same as that employed in coarse fishing and it may well be that unwelcome surprises may be hooked, such as large eels wound round the tackle, instead of the anticipated Sea trout.

Float Fishing with a Worm
I was taught this method of fishing when a youngster and the principle is simple. The worm is thoroughly impaled on the hook, the float is set at the right length so that the worm dangles on or an inch or two above the bottom, and the line is weighted with split shot from about a foot above the hook, sufficient to make the line hang straight and to make the float set up vertically. At the slightest movement of the float the angler should strike, but quite often an eel may quietly eat the worm without visible movement and removing them can be a messy task. Nor is handling worms a task for the squeamish. Good worms should be dug up and selected a day or two before they are required and kept in a convenient tin in moss to toughen. Alternatively, extraordinarily good rubber imitations are available.

Unlikely Waters
It is surprising in these post-spate conditions how often large trout, both Brown and Sea trout, may be caught in very unlikely places. A fencer of my acquaintance was clearing a weed-filled ditch with a heavy fork one day just after some heavy flooding. As he waded in the ditch in thigh boots he felt an occasional brushing against his legs through the rubber. Thrusting downwards with his fork to see what was causing this he was surprised to impale a 3 to 4 pound Sea trout, which he hoiked onto the bank. His 'bag' by the end of the day amounted to three Sea trout and two Brown trout of similar proportions. A worm employed in such circumstances would have probably produced a vastly larger bag, but then this is not fishing in the accepted meaning of the word; it is simply pulling fish out of the water, and where still permissible, should be made illegal for the greater benefit of both fish and anglers.

Spinning for Sea Trout

Especially in tidal waters, spinning for Sea trout can be positively deadly, but requires virtually none of the skill involved in fly fishing. Mechanically reeling the fish in with the slipping clutch set to maintain constant pressure also removes all the skill involved in playing the fish. It is important to reel in the bait or lure very fast in order to entice Sea trout, but, that said, there is little real satisfaction involved in catching them by this means compared with using a fly. When all else has failed, however, it may be permissible to turn to the spinning rod to see whether there are any fish in the water. On such occasions spinning may be the only means of catching a Sea trout, but when they are coming at every cast the spinning rod should be put aside and the fly rod used instead.

The Cannibal

If there is one thing that is certain it is that not all trout in the same area will necessarily behave in the same way. There are, for instance, some trout who are persistent bottom feeders, who seldom seem to come to the surface for a change of diet. Then again there are those who have become persistent cannibals, surviving largely on their own kind. As they grow larger it is possible that some trout become accustomed largely to bottom feeding, starting by living largely on small crustacea and graduating from them to minnows and to small species of their own kind. Such trout naturally find that they do better by living deeper and nearer the bottom.

The Ferox

The Ferox probably has some similarities to the species in Ireland known as the Gillaroo, although that feeds largely on molluscs. It is suggested it is nothing more than a cannibal trout in surroundings which have encouraged the development of those cannibal tendencies. Ferox are generally only to be found in lochs where there are shoals of char. The char live some 20 to 30 feet below the surface, only occasionally coming nearer the surface in the summer months. Starting as ordinary cannibal trout, the theory is that the Ferox finally discover the char, and in course of time take to inhabiting the depths beneath their prey. In the process they grow extremely large and frequently also extremely ugly, often with malformed head, and large, hooked jaws and a lank, lean body. It is only fair to add that sometimes Ferox can also be quite handsome, well-developed beasts, but of considerable size ranging from 10 or so to over 20 pounds.

Fishing for Ferox

Fishing for Ferox even in waters where they are known to exist is usually a somewhat hit and miss affair. They are generally caught by trolling with minnows sunk deeply behind a dinghy being systematically rowed up and down the deeper sections of a suitable loch. Two spinning rods are normally used, each pointing outwards from the stern of the boat with a long line of around 40 or 50 yards let out. The speed of the bait should be varied by rowing slower or faster, and the depth at which it is fished should also be varied by altering the weights being used to sink the bait, until the right combination is found. Deep water spinning with a large minnow, in waters where they are likely to be found, would also seem to be a promising way of catching them. Since they are themselves likely to be mainly interested in char the chances are that they will be found in those particular areas of the loch where the shoals of char are likely to be encountered. The angler who goes after Ferox therefore has to work on several assumptions: first, that there are Ferox in the water being fished; secondly, that the right area has been selected, for clearly such fish are likely to be loners, each with its own territory; thirdly, that they will be in the mood for taking the bait and fourthly, that the chosen bait is of suitable size and attraction and is being fished at the correct depth. There are a lot of assumptions involved, which may explain why few anglers seriously go out in search of Ferox and why only occasional specimens are caught.

CHAPTER EIGHT

Mainly Lochs, Lakes and Reservoirs

Fishing from the Bank
Small Lochs or Lakes for Wild Brown Trout

If these have been put first it is because they usually provide me with my favourite fishing. To begin with access may be difficult, requiring a lengthy walk across difficult country carrying one's gear. On one's arrival the water itself may look unpromising, with weedy, unkempt edges and nothing very much visible in the way of fish. A floating line and a cast of standard loch flies is probably all that is required. The likely fishing spots are soon discovered and in the course of a day most of the water can probably be covered. The fish themselves are often obligingly ingenuous, unaccustomed to an array of artificial flies, and on occasions may take freely even when the fly presented to them is totally unlike anything they are currently feeding on or are accustomed to seeing. The fish may be small by the standards of put-and-take fisheries, but the sport can often be considerable, especially when there is a natural rise, and a self-imposed bag limit will always leave the angler with a feeling of virtue rewarded after a lengthy day in wild surroundings.

Small Artificially-Stocked Lakes

In small fisheries, possibly with an artificially-excavated lake, there is very often no great problem in catching trout. Whether they are stocked with Brown trout, American Brook trout, or Rainbow trout, or all three, is immaterial. Some of the larger of these fish may be experienced in rejecting artificial flies and lures, having been subjected to a considerable variety during their sojourn in the lake and possibly even having been hooked, played and returned in the past, or else having escaped on several occasions and learned by their past mistakes. These cunning larger trout are likely to be found in the depths of the lake and will not be readily caught with the more obvious lures or flies. They are also likely to be solitary, rather than swimming in shoals, as do so many of the more recently introduced fish.

Ringing the Changes

On such artificially-stocked waters it is advisable to start with a floating line but be ready to change over to a sinking line if the first approach is unproductive. Using a cast of nymphs on the floating line, and retrieving them slowly with a twitch of the rod point whenever any slight movement on the line is seen, will usually prove successful on some innocents. If, however, there is no success with this method it should be worth changing to a sinking line, and shrimp on the tail and a couple of sedge flies on the droppers. This should be a quick sinker if the water appears deep, but a slow sinker if it seems shallow. The depth at which either is fished should be varied until some success is achieved, if only a sign of movement. If nothing is doing with this method then change the flies and try again, but in most fisheries the regular alteration of fishing methods will sooner or later start catching fish and it should not be difficult to reach the bag limit.

Fishing the Larger Water

Whether the larger water is stocked with Rainbows or other trout, or whether it only contains wild Brown trout, some degree of local knowledge is invaluable. Without this the angler who is faced with a large expanse of water is always under a considerable handicap. When fishing from a boat the same handicap exists, but when fishing from the bank there are severe limits on where one can fish. It is probably best initially to try a rod with a floating rather than a sinking line for most of the year when the fish are feeding near the surface, although a sinking line on a spare reel is always essential to have in reserve. Fishing at an angle to the bank into the prevailing wind is likely to provide the best chance, since feed will be blown towards the bank and fish may be feeding quite close in. Any promontories, jetties, small bays, or streams entering the water are always worth investigation, and are likely to prove worthwhile. To stay in one place is unlikely to prove fruitful, but rather than keeping constantly on the move, time spent in likely looking spots is always worthwhile. On finding likely places they should be well fished then possibly revisited. In this way there is more chance of success than flogging unlikely water to no avail. Of course, where the water is well stocked there will usually (on the face of it) be more likelihood of catching fish, but the wild Browns may be less sophisticated and will usually be more widely distributed than the Rainbows or other introductions. It is unwise therefore to assume that in large waters the one which is artificially-stocked will necessarily provide more sport. It is always exasperating to see fish rising near islands or in areas it is impossible to reach from the bank. There can be no doubt that fishing from a boat in such circumstances does allow a much greater freedom of movement, but this is not to say that bank fishing is not often highly profitable and can provide not only good sport but a good bag. Very often the fish are feeding close in to the shore and a careful approach and the right choice of fly can result in a highly satisfactory day's sport.

Speed of Fishing Retrieve
The speed with which flies or bait are retrieved can be of immense importance. I have known anglers who retrieved their flies very fast and often caught fish, but in general it is not a good idea to retrieve line too fast. It is usually only those innocent trout recently introduced into a fishery which will take a fly dragged across the surface at speed. The fact that they do take almost anything at times is capable of deceiving some people into believing that this is the way to fish, but when they come to try their hand at wild Browns, or experienced trout, they will learn that these are a different matter altogether. A steady draw to keep the line just taut without any slack is usually correct. An occasional slight jerk of the line held in the left hand or of the rod tip to give the flies a certain enticing movement is usually well worthwhile, but this too can be overdone. A great deal depends on circumstances such as light, ripple, wind, speed of drift in a boat, depth of the flies, water temperature and so on. It is never wise to be too dogmatic

about such matters since what seems to catch fish one day may fail utterly in seemingly similar circumstances on another.

Speed and Behaviour of Natural Feed
It is only necessary to watch minnows, or trout fingerlings, moving in shallow water to realise that it is not desirable to retrieve any lure steadily without stops and starts. These tiny fish will move in a short quick dash, then halt and possibly change direction. The wet fly which is imitating them should be retrieved in short jerks, with occasional sideways movements of the rod tip and tweaks on the line from the left hand. There should be short pauses when no movement is made at all and the line is allowed to sink once again, like a nymph struggling to the surface. The rod tip should not remain static all the time, but criss-cross movements, not fast in themselves, may be very helpful in imitating the natural movements of nymph or minnow.

Fishing Depths
The essence of good fishing practice is always to consider alternatives and to try them out where possible. Thus, even if you seem to be catching trout well at a certain depth, and with a cast of certain flies, it is well worth trying the same flies at greater depths and possibly even changing them. The results can sometimes be surprisingly good. In some fisheries, for instance, there may be small eager takers, recently introduced, taking near the surface whereas by fishing deeper and with different flies, or even the same ones, larger fish introduced the previous season may be taken which have in the course of time discovered better feeding in the depths, in the manner of Ferox in the early stages.

Floating Line
It is surprising to me that so many people unquestioningly use a light coloured floating line when green or brown coloured floating lines are as readily available. It seems to me logical that if a fish can see a figure against the skyline and may be startled by the sight of nylon flashing, as they undoubtedly can be, then they must also be able to see

a white line against the water, and once they associate this with an angler it must be cause for alarm. I have not witnessed it myself, but the presence of a white floating line has been seen to startle fish, and personally I am prepared to accept that willingly enough. It seems perfectly logical that this should be so and why set out to handicap oneself when it is not necessary to do so.

Still Water
On the face of it still water is simply water without a current flowing through it. This term therefore covers all artificial lakes and reservoirs and most natural lochs and lakes throughout the country. Fishing such waters as has been noted, is termed stillwater angling, but virtually exactly the same methods of fishing are employed in lochs or lakes open to the sea, or those with a river running into them at one end and running out at the other, or in many cases in rivers and in burns or streams. That there may be differences implicit in the nature of things when there is a current acting on the flies or bait is true enough, but there is not really a great deal of difference in practice between the various forms of fishing, or perhaps, to be more accurate, similar methods with minor differences in technique and application are generally effective in all waters. This remains true whether fishing a sea loch in the highlands, a chalk stream in Hampshire, a rocky stream in Devon, or a reservoir in Wales.

The Benefits of Experience
There may well be, however, a world of difference between the fish to be found in each of these differing waters and how they react. Therein lies the real contrast, although their different size or appearance is not the principal factor involved. The skill of the angler may well be tried to the full in each case and sometimes very different techniques have to be employed to be successful: but sometimes identical methods will work under quite different circumstances. It is necessary to try to work out what problems each new water is likely to produce and to do this reasonably well the only solution is to gain experience and draw on it. Each new water fished should

provide some fresh nugget of information which may be of use in another outing.

Lochs and Lakes
The size of a loch or lake is no measure of its fishing qualities. Some are deep right from the edge, almost wedge shaped with considerable depths in the centre, whereas others are comparatively shallow throughout. In general the latter are to be preferred, although water with islands and contrasting depths, such as Loch Lomond or many Irish loughs, can provide extremely varied and interesting fishing.

Reservoirs
Since the 1950s there has been a great increase in the numbers of reservoirs in this country and the ever increasing demand for water and for power from hydro-electric schemes resulting from the steady growth of our towns and cities has caused many of those already built to be enlarged or greatly altered. This, in turn, has resulted in most of these man-made waters being available for fishing. Unlike many of the natural lochs, or lakes, which tend to be narrow and deep, most of the reservoirs sited in the low-lying Midland counties are wide, with bays and shallow inlets around the edges, providing excellent fishing facilities for both boat and bank anglers. Some of the higher Pennine reservoirs, however are nearly as deep-sided as the lakes, or lochs, formed by glaciers which are found in many of the mountainous parts of Scotland and Wales.

Stillwater Angling
As indicated above there is usually some flow to be found even in man-made reservoirs, where the outlet flow may be pumped out through a lengthy piped system. There are almost always feeder streams coming at various angles, quite naturally following the contours of the hills. Although the flow may be so slow as to be almost negligible the streams inevitably bring food in their current into the reservoir or lake, and trout will gather round these sources of feeding, just as they will gather wherever

feeding is available, as for instance under overhanging bushes where natural feed may be found, or where the prevailing wind drives food ashore. The lake, loch or reservoir angler looks for all these likely places where fish may be lying, in the same way that the river angler looks for likely pools, backwaters, eddies and rocks, where fish are likely to be sheltering out of the main current. With each new water fished fresh experience is gained.

The Differences Between Lochs, Lakes and Reservoirs

The main difference between these waters from an angler's viewpoint, as with rivers, is the amount of feeding available for trout. As has been seen, some fast flowing shallow rivers have little feed for trout whereas others flowing slowly through rich agricultural land have plenty of feeding available. The lakes, lochs and reservoirs in rich agricultural areas tend to have more feeding available than those in bare mountainous regions. Similarly steep-sided deep lochs, lakes and reservoirs tend to provide poorer feeding than shallower basins of water where the water temperature is also likely to be higher thus encouraging the growth of natural feed. Where there is much settled agriculture with plentiful and rich mineral salts flowing into the water from the catchment area, the diet of the trout, particularly the minute plankton, their natural feed, is greatly enhanced. Weed growth, as in some rivers, may be luxuriant in the shallows of such waters and will need cutting back to make fishing possible. Alternatively in the summer months, the growth of plankton and plant life may be so great as to deprive the water of oxygen. This can in extreme cases lead in turn to the death of fish through lack of oxygen.

The Effects of Contours and Weather

In some large lakes, lochs or reservoirs it is possible to have one end steeply sloping and narrow with the other end forming a comparatively shallow basin, so that the two different types of fishing are to be found in the different ends of the one area of water. Loch Lomond is a classic example of this with the northern end steep-sided and narrow while the southern end opens up into a comparatively shallow, island-studded basin. The effects of the weather in such circumstances can be dramatic with a wind funnelling down from the north quite fiercely at the northern end but merely a fresh breeze by the time it reaches the southern end. With islands, bays and inlets providing shelter there are always places where fish may be caught. To fish the exposed water in such circumstances would be both difficult and pointless. As with all fishing it is up to the angler to make the most of the choices that are present in different circumstances.

Fishing from a Boat

Apart from avoiding needless noise in a boat, which is very clearly transmitted via the water to the fish, it is also advisable to avoid standing and casting a shadow in front, just as when standing on the bank. Standing up in a boat in any case is always undesirable because it is easy to make an incautious move and either fall overboard, or capsize. In clear water the shadow of the boat, and even the shadow of movement, is enough to set trout scattering. When chosing the drift it is, as pointed out, a good thing to take the line where the water deepens so that one can fish at varying depths and cover ground not easily reached from the bank. At the same time it must be appreciated that very often the fish are in fact lying close in to the bank. From a boat, of course, it is easy enough to cast over such trout without frightening them.

Fishing from the Bank of Larger Waters

It must seem obvious to anyone who has read as far as this that to stand on the bank near the car park of any large reservoir, loch or lake, without stirring from the spot, and possibly flanked by 20, 30, or even more other anglers all busily casting, is not likely to be very productive. Yet the fact remains that numerous innocents will be seen at any fishery where bank fishing is permitted doing just that. The larger the water the further it generally pays to walk from others. Paying attention to places where fish are likely to be found, such as promontories and points where feeder streams enter, be they only very minor ones, is likely to pay dividends.

Regularly Stocked Fisheries

Where a fishery is very frequently re-stocked, especially with Rainbows, the fish are inclined to swim in shoals. Initially some are likely to remain relatively close to where they were placed in the water before dispersing. Some, however, especially the larger Rainbows, tend to head for deeper water and may be found here waiting for their regular twice-daily rations of feeding pellets to appear in the manner to which they are accustomed. Only when they realise that they may now have to forage for natural food will they desert the deeper water and be found in shallower areas. In such waters these innocent fish may often be readily enticed with some outlandish flies and lures.

CHAPTER NINE

Mainly Small Rivers

A Question of Size

Quite when a stream, or burn, becomes a river is open to question, but for the angler there is not a great deal of difference between them. It is only when the river becomes so large that a boat is required to fish it properly that the matter becomes somewhat different, and by then it is often more properly termed an estuary. The small stream and the larger river are frequently similar to each other in the way they bend and twist and it is often only in size and scale that they differ greatly. Yet, at the same time, rivers in various parts of any country may differ greatly from each other. The mountain stream or highland river subject to flash floods is as different from the quiet chalk stream meandering through lush water meadows as a hornet from a bumble bee, but each can provide splendid fishing for the enthusiast if approached in the correct manner.

Small Streams and Burns

What in the south may be termed a brook, and in the north a burn, is frequently ignored as not likely to produce any interesting trout fishing, yet this can often be a very great mistake. Even where the rod itself can reach right across from bank to bank without any need to cast there may be some interesting fishing to be had. The scale may be smaller all round. An average trout may be no more than a quarter or half a pound and a monster will possibly reach a full pound, but such small streams can still provide interesting fishing, mirroring in every respect their larger counterparts. The angler who starts as a youngster in just such a small stream or burn will find later that the larger river and the larger trout are in no way different. They can even be less wary and easier to catch. The sport involved in catching a basket of wild Brown half-pounders may be every bit as great and even more enjoyable than that involved in catching carefully reared Rainbows four times the size in a stretch of preserved water on a well known river; furthermore they will probably taste a great deal better. It is never wise to ignore any water however unpromising it may seem at first sight, and to try to assess it by size alone is a great mistake.

Fishing the Small Stream or Burn
As will have been gathered such waters can be enormous fun to fish as well as providing exciting sport. It is, of course, necessary to think on a smaller scale, where, as indicated, the quarter or half pound Brown trout is the average and a three-quarter or full pounder is exceptional. The $9^1/2$ feet rod may be far too large and even $8\ ^1/2$ feet may be more than enough. Here the approach is all important, and each individual trout may be seen and stalked, using any cover provided by bank, or bush, even sometimes approaching on hands and knees, possibly forcing one's way through overhanging bushes and casting in unorthodox ways to get the fly on the water in the desired spot. The line may need to be cast out with what can only be described as a sideways twitch of the rod to land it in front of a monster of a pound or more. Mostly this will be dry fly fishing, although on occasions a wet fly may be used, or even a nymph. It is in such upland burns that upstream worming and guddling are often practised successfully.

Upstream Worming
Quite often in these confined waters it will be found that upstream worming, a method of fishing very akin to upstream nymphing, with a worm in place of the nymph, is the best method available. Do not let anyone be misled into thinking this is sport to be despised simply because it is on a smaller scale than that to which they are accustomed. Nor should the use of a worm in such circumstances be regarded as beneath contempt. The skill required is every bit as great and very similar indeed to that in upstream nymphing. Once the worm has been threaded successfully onto a hook of the required size it may be cast upstream. Then the line must be kept taut as

it is slowly retrieved and at the slightest sign of tension the rod tip must be raised and the strike made. When the individual fish may be seen inspecting the bait there is a natural urge to strike too soon and it is probable that on first trying this method of fishing the average angler will make a very poor showing. It is, however, well worth persevering.

Guddling

Although it may seem to some inappropriate to describe guddling trout in a book on fishing there must be many who have started their fishing days on small waters in this way, and benefited greatly from the knowledge of trout they have gained thereby. Quite simply guddling consists of feeling extremely gently under stones, or in similar lies where trout may be found, and on feeling the fish grasping them firmly. There is a natural reaction to the clammy feel of the fish on first contact which may cause the novice to react by letting go rather than grasping the trout, but with perseverance this can be overcome. My youngest daughter, once taught, became unusually expert, capable on occasions of reaching both hands under a stone where she knew trout to be lying and coming up with one in each hand. On our nearby burn she would frequently return after an hour or so with a bag of 15-20 delicious little half-pounders. In fact she was doing the water a service by preventing it from becoming overstocked with under-sized trout.

Knowledge Gained by Observation

A knowledge of the ways of water and how the river flows, the depths and underwater snags, and the likely haunts of trout, are important to any river fisherman, and much can be learned by following the course of a stream and examining the way in which the action of floodwater has formed its course, undercutting the bank in one place and carving out a deep pool in another, while the effect of a fallen tree or boulder provides a natural lie for trout in yet another place. Such elements in a minor stream or tributary are usually to be found repeated on a larger scale in the parent river itself.

Careful observation of any river when the water is low will repay the angler many times over.

Worming

It is easy to be totally contemptuous of worming and there is no doubt that spate worming is a deadly and unsporting method of catching a sporting fish, being rightly barred in many waters in England. In Scotland, Ireland, Wales and Devon the worm is often used in small muddy upland burns, or streams, but there are certain points which should be borne in mind. First, when the water is muddy and rising the trout are only likely to take a worm in the first half hour or so of the rising water. After that they probably look for cover and are unlikely to take again until the water has reached its peak. They may then start taking once more, but while there is any further rise in the water, or while it is receding they will not take readily. Until the river level has settled they are unlikely to take anything, even a worm.

The Worming Technique

It is easy enough to make a considerable bag worming, but even here the novice can go badly wrong. The worm that is fresh from under a stone will probably prove too tender to use and it is better kept in a moss filled tin box for a day or two, when it will have become much tougher. The places to fish are the sheltered eddies and pools out of the mainstream, where the worm can be kept under control and is not readily swept away. The line should be well weighted to allow the worm to hang direct. Direct contact should always be kept with the worm so that a strike may be made at the first sign of contact. Otherwise it is only too easy to strike and find the worm gone and no trout present. While large bags are easily enough made with practice the novice may not immediately be successful. For the angler after Sea trout the worm may represent the only chance of sport, until the water has cleared enough to use a spinning bait, since they are likely to run upstream during a flood. Regardless of circumstances, however, no one with an ounce of sportsmanship would wish to make a large bag in such circumstances when the odds are unfairly weighted against the trout.

Clear-Water Worming

Upstream clear-water worming, as indicated above, is a deadly method of fishing when performed by an expert, but requires quite as much skill, if not even more in its way, as upstream nymphing. The normal procedure is to use a long rod of some 12 feet, with a light line and a light cast. A little split shot is sometimes used, but in fact the weight of the worm is usually enough to let the worm roll along the bottom of the burn, or stream. A short worm of 1 1/2 inches at most is best, so that there is not too much which can be taken by the trout without danger of being hooked. The worm is not cast, but is gently swung forward on a line no longer than the length of the rod. The fisherman is wading quietly up the centre of the burn and as he swings the rod forward the rod tip nearly touches the water. It is then raised steadily as the worm trundles back towards the angler in the current with the line kept taut the whole time. At any hesitation, at any gleam of silver scales, or if there is the slightest tug the angler should lower the rod slightly and tighten the line gently by turning the rod point downstream horizontally. A good bag requires considerable delicacy of touch.

Ideal Conditions

This sort of worming is best conducted in sunny conditions in dead low water, with the surface of the water slightly ruffled by a breeze. The most successful anglers will be those who learned to guddle when young, for they will know exactly where to expect the trout to lie. In that this form of fishing probably tests the knowledge of where to find fish almost as much as guddling it is worth trying at least once, although not much success can be expected on the early outings. It is a much underrated sport which requires a lot of practice, but given the right surroundings and the right state of mind it can provide as good a day's enjoyment as most other forms of fishing and should certainly not be condemned untried. The novice will find it surprisingly difficult to master.

Fishing with a Maggot

This is very similar to worm fishing from the bank. Trout may sometimes be caught with surprising baits, even pieces of bread and baked beans have been effective at times on curious and incautious newly-stocked fish. Maggots are something I do not care to handle unduly having seen them too often at work in animal and, come to that, human flesh. They are, however, very effective given the right conditions and as such are rightly banned in many waters. They are easily produced by letting a fly breed in any meat left in the open. They will develop in hot weather within a week. Frozen they will remain static for weeks. Left outside they pupate into a brownish torpedo-shaped object. This is a useful bait, if unpleasant to handle. Some float and some do not, so that they can be used either sunk or on the surface. At one time it was popular to dye maggots, but the dyes proved to be extremely carcinogenic. They are a deadly enough bait without such additions.

Using a Spinning Rod for Bait

Although not generally associated with bait or fly fishing, it is of course always possible to use a bubble float and some lead to cast a spinning line baited with either wet flies, or with anything from worms to maggots, far into selected waters. When then gently reeled in, this can be a deadly form of what can only be described as poaching, since it requires little or no skill and in most waters its use is almost certainly and rightly illegal. Using a cast of wet flies in this way is, of course, very similar to the old poaching method of using an otter board and a line of flies, something like the naval use of a paravane against mines, towed on the end of a rope. It is rightly illegal.

The Reasons for Fishing

It is quite important to appreciate that an angler is not necessarily a patient man. In fact patience has very little to do with angling, unless it is the kind required for undoing a monumental tangle of line. The impatient angler will simply cut it and replace it with fresh line, or continue with a reduced length. The reasons for fishing are that to be successful it requires and demands complete concentration. When there is a chance a fish may rise to the fly at any moment, and may not be hooked unless you are concentrating on it fully, it is impossible to think about bank balances, mortgages, take-overs and other mundane matters. It is this necessity to subordinate the mind to the task in hand which makes fishing both absorbing and refreshing to the keen angler.

Fishing with Explosives
There has to be some degree of effort involved in fishing and this is so even when using explosives. Simply throwing a stick of gelignite into a well-stocked pool is beneath contempt, but on occasions even the use of explosives might be excusable. Needing a change of diet from never-ending bully beef, I once tried swimming into the Mediterranean close to Algiers with a hand grenade primed in each hand. Some 25 yards out I threw one after another then turned and swam for the shore until they exploded. Returning to the site of the detonations I found several large fish floating stunned on the surface. With one under each arm I then did my best backstroke for the shore and although one escaped I did return with one large struggling fish for dinner.

Even compared with this, the Maharajah's method simply cannot be considered sporting fishing. It is neither time consuming nor does it require concentration. There is no effort involved, the odds are unduly weighted against the fish, and there should be no satisfaction either.

Satisfaction Gained
Fishing should never be too easy. Those anglers who simply stand close to the car park of the fishery, flogging the water, shoulder to shoulder, may catch their bag limit of reared trout, and if they are satisfied with that so, no doubt, is the fishery manager. The effort involved in walking over the hills and catching a bagful of wild Brown trout may be considerable and the total weight of the catch may not be as great as that caught in a commercial fishery, even with a bag limit, but the sport enjoyed and the satisfaction gained is surely not to be compared. In all sport the amount of satisfaction and enjoyment gained should be at least to

some extent proportionate to the amount of time and effort expended, and angling is no exception. The more anglers come to rely on fisheries to provide them with artificial fishing, the more artificial their sport will become. It is tempting indeed to go along to an artificial lake close at hand where large fish may be comparatively easily hooked and caught, but it is also the line of least resistance.

Acknowledging a Debt

The angler who feels that fishing has provided him, or her, with hours of satisfactory relaxation should be prepared to do something in return. Apart from ensuring that no gates are left open, or other rules of the countryside broken, and that no spare pieces of nylon, empty beer cans, plastic bags, or other detritus are left behind after a day's fishing, it is also important to fight any danger to the sport. Pollution in countless forms, by insecticides, by farm sprays, by oil spillage and in many other ways can damage fishing immeasurably. There are also those who would stop all field sports, from hunting and shooting through to fishing. It is up to every angler to fight these threats and give their support to any cause supporting these aims or their sport will ultimately be endangered.

Effort Well Spent

To find places where wild, or comparatively wild, trout may be caught may involve greater expense and effort. The trout may not be easily caught even then. That, however, is precisely the sort of effort which makes fishing worthwhile. If the stage is ever reached where all the wild fish have died of disease and trout can only be caught in artificial waters where they have been hand reared, the greater part of the pleasure to be had from fishing will have disappeared. By that time, no doubt, all the natural flies will also have been eradicated by insecticides and all the natural waters irretrievably polluted. It is not a world any sporting angler would care to inhabit. Nevertheless, in the meantime wherever and however you may fish, tight lines.

Recipes

Cooking Trout

It is surprising how often keen anglers either know nothing, or care less, about the preparation of trout for the table. Even many fishing inns seem incapable of cooking the fish on which their reputation depends. To my mind this is a shame and any angler worth the name should be able to cook the fish he catches.

The Small Trout

For a small trout of under a pound the best way of cooking is undoubtedly in oatmeal. After gutting and cleaning, dry it and brush with beaten egg. Then dip it in fine or medium oatmeal and crisp fry it in deep fat for about eight minutes. Serve with a large slice of lemon as garnish. Squeeze the lemon over it before eating and there is no better way of eating trout of that size for breakfast, or indeed, at any meal.

The Larger Trout

For a trout of from one to two pounds or more the best method of cooking, in my view is baking. Prepare the trout by gutting, cleaning and removing the head and tail to reduce the size if necessary, then dry it and cut shallow slantwise incisions, just breaking the skin, at around inch intervals down both sides. Sprinkle both sides with salt and pepper and brush liberally with melted butter. Then place in an oven at around 350 degree to 400 degrees F until cooked. Then serve with a sliced cucumber or meuniere sauce. This is superb.

Glossary of Terms

Amadou An absorbent fungus used to dry the fly when it loses buoyancy through becoming wet when dry fly fishing. Now largely replaced by various patent water-repellent sprays or floatants.

Backing A cheaper line used on a fishing reel below the principal line, but spliced on to it to provide a safe margin in the event of a large fish taking out a great deal of line.

Belly Of a line, to float in a curve between the rod point and the fly or flies, causing them to react unnaturally.

Blood Knot A knot used to join different lengths of nylon securely.

Bob The description used for the top dropper on a wet fly cast, so-named because it tends to bob on the surface film of the water in an attractive manner. Hence, bob fly.

Bulging Rise The bulge on the surface caused by a fish feeding on flies or nymphs beneath the surface of the water.

Cast (or Leader) The length of tapered nylon between the line on the reel and the artificial fly.

Chironimids Midges.

Close Season The period when fishing is not allowed, when the fish are breeding and in poor condition, which may vary from March to October with considerable local variations.

Dap To fish by letting the fly bounce lightly on the surface of the water using the wind to carry the line.

Double taper line A line with a taper at each end providing double life.

Drag The movement of the artificial fly on the water when there is belly on the line caused by the current affecting the line adversely.

Drift The line chosen to be covered when allowing a boat to drift down a loch, lake or reservoir in front of the wind; on the chosen line depends much of the success of the day.

Dropper The fly, or flies, attached to a wet fly cast by a 3 inch length of nylon.

Dry Fly An artificial fly designed to float attractively on the surface film of the water.

Dun A fly which has emerged from the nymphal stage prior to making its first flight.

Ephemeridae A class of fly of great interest and importance to the angler: see life cycle of aquatic fly.

Ferrule The joint of metal or plastic, or similar material, used to join the various jointed sections of a fishing rod. They have male and female suction joints.

Fly Box A box designed especially for holding flies.

Fly Rod A rod especially designed for fly fishing.

Hook The semi-circular and usually barbed piece of steel on which the fly is tied. The scale of measurement used for trout hooks is generally known as the New Scale.

Landing Net Net used for landing fish.

Leader (or Cast) see *Cast*.

Mending the Line Raising the rod tip and, by a quick movement reversing the belly on the line caused by the current thus removing the drag on the line.

Nylon A synthetic material used by anglers for cast and for spinning lines, which should be renewed annually and should never be left lying about.

Nymph The larval stage of aquatic insects.

Playing the Fish Maintaining the maximum strain consistent with the strength of the tackle.

Priest A weighted club for killing fish humanely when landed.

Rod The thin balanced length of wood, or other material, to which the reel and line are attached, with which the angler casts his fly and plays the fish.

Rod rings The rings attached to the rod through which the line runs freely, both in casting and in playing the fish.

Sneck Of a hook, the sideways bend sometimes to be found in certain types of hook.

Still water Any area of water with no obvious current running through it, e.g. any loch, lake or reservoir.

Strike The action of raising the rod point, or tightening the line, to drive the hook home into the trout's jaw when it is seen to take the fly.

Tackle All apparatus associated with angling.

Trout (Brown) A freshwater game fish commonly found throughout the UK.

Trout (Rainbow) A freshwater game fish introduced to this country from California and now widely used to stock private waters of all kinds. Common to most fish farms.

Turle Knot A knot used for attaching the fly to the cast.

Worm Fly A dark Palmer fly mounted in tandem with two bodies and two hooks, but only one eye. Mostly used under trees, or bushes, where trout may be feeding on caterpillars.

Recommended Further Reading

Brander, Michael. *Trout Fishing*. Edinburgh: 1981.

Buller, F. and Falkus, Hugh. *Freshwater Fishing*. London: 1975.

Cass, A.R.H. *Catching the Wily Sea Trout*. London: 1943.

Currie, W.B. *Trout Fishing*. Edinburgh: 1961.

Falkus, Hugh. *Sea Trout Fishing*. London: 1975.

Goddard, J. *Trout Fly Recognition*. London: 1966.

Greenhalgh, Malcolm. *Lake, Loch and Reservoir Fishing*. London: 1987.

Hills, J.W. *A History of Fly Fishing for Trout*. London: 1921

Horsley, Terence. *Fishing and Flying*. London: 1947.

Ivens, T.C. *Stillwater Fly-Fishing*. London: 1973.

Macdonald Robertson. R. *Wade the River Drift the Loch*. Edinburgh: 1948.

Pearson, Alan. *An Introduction to Reservoir Trout Fishing*. London: 1984.

Sawyer, Frank. *Nymphs and the Trout*. London: 1970.

Skues, G.E.M. *Nymph Fishing for Chalk Stream Trout*. London: 1939.

Turing, H.D. *Trout Fishing*. London: 1943.

Wilson, Dermot. *Dry Fly Beginnings*. London: 1957